Sarah Faulkner's
Planning a Home
Projects Manual

Karen Gustafson Bromberg

Holt, Rinehart and Winston

New York   Chicago   San Francisco   Atlanta

Dallas   Montreal   Toronto   London   Sydney

Editor Rita Gilbert
Picture Editor Joan Curtis
Developmental Editor Karen Dubno
Project Editor Karen Mugler
Production Assistant Barbara Curiallc
Production Manager Nancy Myers
Illustrator Sandra E. Popovich
Associate Illustrators Richard N. Pollack, A.I.A.; Vantage Art, Inc.
Designer Karen Salsgiver

Publisher Judith L. Rothman

The line illustrations and special halftone combinations in this book
were conceived by Joan Curtis and executed by Sandra E. Popovich.

Figures on pp. 66, 67 adapted from *Nomadic Furniture* by James Hennessey
and Victor Papanek. Copyright © 1973 by Victor J. Papanek and James Hennessey.
Adapted by permission of Pantheon Books, a Division of Random House, Inc.

ISBN 0-03-045476-X

Composition by Lexigraphics, Inc., New York
Printing and binding by Edwards Brothers, Michigan
0 1 2 3 4 005 9 8 7 6 5 4 3 2 1

Preface

This Projects Manual is intended for laboratory courses in interior design at the beginning level. It has been designed for use in conjunction with a basic textbook, such as Faulkner's *Planning a Home* (Holt, Rinehart and Winston, 1979) or Faulkner and Faulkner's *Inside Today's Home* (Holt, Rinehart and Winston, 1975). However, if certain background information were supplied by the instructor in class, the Projects Manual could be used independently.

The 45 projects included in the manual represent far more work than could be accomplished in one semester of class time. This has been done deliberately. The availability of a large number of projects allows the instructor (or the student) to choose those that are most interesting and beneficial.

It is suggested that the projects in Section 1 (Planning for People) and Section 2 (Planning for Space) be done first. These two sections provide information and teach basic skills—such as drawing plans and elevations—that will be needed for completion of later projects. Beyond this, the projects can be used in any order.

Most of the projects can be done directly on the pages of this manual. In a few cases, where multiple copies of a form or diagram are needed, the student is asked to make photocopies of pages from the manual. Pages 87 to 98 contain standard forms, outlines, charts, and tables for use in various parts of the manual.

While each of the projects has been designed for a learning experience, an attempt has been made to make the exercises interesting—even fun—to do. Interior design is a fascinating subject, and its study should be equally enjoyable.

The following people have made contributions to this book: Allen Tate, Chairman of the Department of Environmental Design at Parsons School of Design; Professor A. Cimonetti, Chairman of the Department of Interior Design at the Fashion Institute of Technology; and Mr. Satya Gupta, teacher in the Department of Architecture, High School of Art and Design, New York City.

Contents

Introduction: Drawing and Presentation

Interior design is above all a visual endeavor. Although it deals in the solid, functional needs of everyday living, a primary concern is usually how a room or home will *look* after it has been designed.

Regardless of whether you plan to design only your own home or you intend to become a professional interior designer, you often will have recourse to pencil, pen, and paper. Designers work constantly with floor plans, sketches, and drawings, in order to test ideas and alternatives. Moreover, drawings help you to visualize your own ideas and to communicate them to others.

This Introduction, then, lists the basic drawing tools and explains their use. Section 2 (p. 10) teaches the mechanics of schematic drawings, floor plans, and elevation. Mastery of simple—but precise—drawing skills will provide you with the key to understanding interior design concepts.

Drawing Tools and Materials

Depending upon your instructor's preferences and the projects to be completed, you will need most of the tools and materials listed below. Some are termed "optional," because they suggest a more professional level of presentation. All the projects can be completed without the "optional" equipment, but these tools do increase efficiency.

T-Square

A T-square is used to draw horizontal lines. It also serves as a guide for the triangle when you are drawing vertical lines. The most convenient T-squares have clear plastic edges that allow you to see the work under the edge. Choose a T-square no longer than your drawing board. Long ones are difficult to work with, and the end away from the head tends to slip. Be sure that the head and blade are rigidly secured. A T-square is worthless if it is not absolutely straight. Try to check the blade for accuracy before buying or using a T-square.

1

Optional	
T-square	technical drawing pen
45° triangle	waterproof black drawing ink
architect's scales	

Necessary	
drawing board or surface	white glue
¼″ scale graph paper—8½ × 11″ pad and ten single sheets 17″ × 22″	scissors
	pocket tape measure
white drawing paper—one pad, 8½ × 11″	plastic templates for drawing furniture, kitchen equipment, and bathroom fixtures in ¼″ scale (⅛″ lettering guides are also helpful)
vellum tracing paper—two pads, 9 × 12″ and 11 × 14″	
clear plastic 12″ ruler	black felt-tip pen
at least three drawing pencils: one hard, one intermediate, and one soft (perhaps 3H, H, and HB)	watercolors
	colored pencils and/or magic markers
	3-ring looseleaf notebook
sandpaper pad and pencil sharpener or pocket knife	3-hole solid white paper (heavy enough to glue clippings on)
pink pearl eraser	
Artgum eraser	twenty notebook dividers
erasing shield with square holes	artist's sketch portfolio, 23 × 31″
½″ drafting tape	illustration board or mat board (as needed)

When drawing with a T-square:

1. Bring the pencil point in contact with the edge of the T-square, and then allow it to touch the paper.

2. Slant your pencil in the direction the line is being drawn. It is important to maintain the same slant and pressure for the length of the line.

3. As you draw, revolve the pencil slowly so that the point will wear evenly.

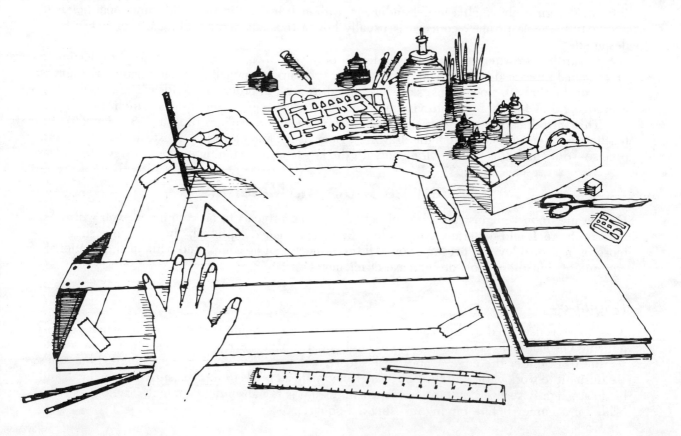

Triangle

Position the triangle against the top edge of the T-square so that the 90° vertical drawing edge will be on the side of the board nearest the T-square's head. Hold the triangle firmly with the same hand that is holding the T-square.

- Draw the line from bottom to top, away from the body.
- Let the pencil lean slightly in the direction in which the line is being drawn.

Graph Paper

A *scale* is a series of spaces marked by lines that represent proportionately larger distances. The scale most frequently used for home plans is ¼″ = 1′. This means that every square foot in your home would be represented by 1 square quarter inch on your paper. The rectangles in the illustration are drawn on ¼″ graph paper. They are marked to show the dimensions of the rooms they represent.

When planning a single room, you may want to choose a somewhat larger scale, perhaps ½″ = 1′, to give you more space to maneuver. It makes no difference, provided *everything* is drawn to the same scale.

The projects in this book suggest ¼″ = 1′ scale. Drawings of that size are convenient to mount on illustration board or mat board. The architectural symbols throughout the book are drawn using ¼″ scale.

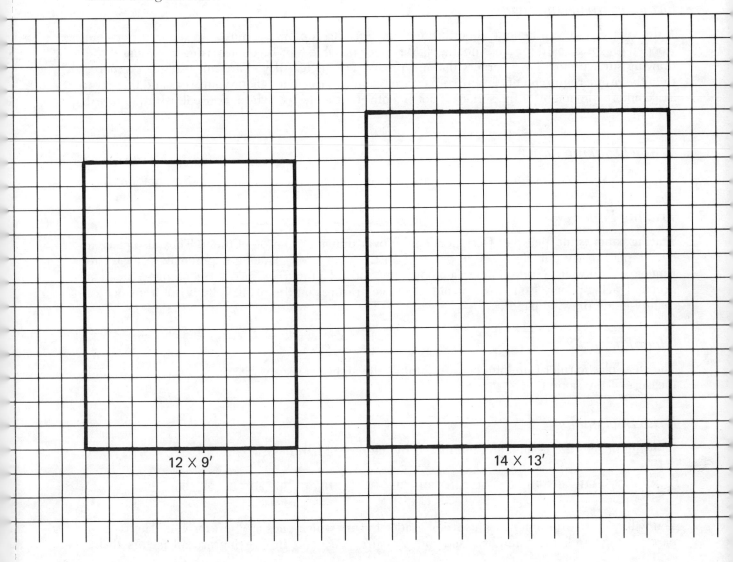

12 X 9′

14 X 13′

Architect's Scales

An architect's scales is a triangular ruler sectioned off in all the commonly used scales, including ¼″ = 1′0 and ½″ = 1′0. It should be used only to measure distances and *not* as a straightedge.

Technical Drawing Pen

Most technical pens have interchangeable tubular points, which make it possible to determine precise line widths. A starting pen set might include the following point sizes:

$$3 \times 0 \text{ produces a .1 mm line}$$
$$2 \times 0 \text{ produces a .2 mm line}$$
$$1 \text{ produces a .4 mm line}$$
$$3 \text{ produces a .8 mm line}$$

Each pen differs in form and operation, but all technical pens must receive special care, since the ink tends to clog and dry in the point. To avoid this, keep points screwed in well, replace the cap after using, and store pens point end up.

Waterproof Black Drawing Ink

Pelican Fount India Ink is a nonclogging ink.

Drawing Board or Surface

A drawing surface can be an elaborate Lucite or Formica top on an adjustable stand, a portable wooden drawing board, or any smooth, rigid surface or table top. If you are using a T-square, the drawing surface must have corners that are precise 90° angles. If you are not using a T-square, then the prime requirements for the surface are that it be large enough for your work and that it be at a comfortable height. If the surface is not smooth, tape a piece of white, dense illustration board over it.

White Drawing Paper

Buy the best drawing paper you can afford. It makes a big difference in your presentation.

Tracing Paper

Tracing paper is inexpensive. Designers tape it over drawings to protect them. They also place it over a plan to try out ideas before drawing on the plan itself. Tracing paper makes it easy to remove or add walls, position the sofa on the other side of a room, or make a rug orange instead of green. Tracing paper also helps to avoid excessive erasures on the plan. Vellum is a translucent, quality-grade drawing paper.

Clear Plastic 12″ Ruler

The clear plastic ruler is helpful because, unlike the architect's scales, it can be used to draw and measure at the same time.

Drawing Pencils

Drawing pencils are graded and numbered by degrees of hardness:

	9H	8H	7H	6H	5H	4H	3H	2H	H	F	HB	B	2B	3B	4B	5B	6B	
hardest																		softest

You will need to experiment with several grades to find which ones are best for you. The type of paper being used, the humidity, and the pressure you exert in drawing are all factors to be considered. Rougher paper requires harder lead, and high humidity makes the lead seem harder. Grades 4H to 2H are commonly used for layout work and detailing, H and F for darkening wall lines, and HB for lettering. Another consideration is how accurate your drawings need to be. Harder leads are more accurate and smudge less easily, but they are also more difficult to erase. If your drawings are to be reproduced, softer leads are more opaque and reproduce better. Grade HB is the softest lead you should ever use on a plan.

Sandpaper Pad, Pencil Sharpener, Pocket Knife

Pencil sharpeners can be used, but some do not give a sharp point. Many artists remove the wood with a pocket knife and rotate the lead on a piece of sandpaper. When rubbing the pencil lead on the sandpaper, hold the pencil at a low angle to achieve the correct taper. Use the sandpaper often.

Erasers

The *pink pearl* eraser is pink rubber: its narrow tip is convenient for erasing dark lines in small spaces. The *Artgum* eraser is soft and block-shaped. It is used to clean the background of a drawing, not to erase lines. The Artgum should be rubbed on a piece of scrap paper to clean it before touching it to the drawing.

Erasing Shield

An erasing shield has square holes to isolate the portion to be erased. Place the shield on the drawing, and position it so that an opening is over the area to be erased. Rub the area with the eraser. It is also helpful to have a soft brush with which to brush away the eraser crumbs.

Drafting Tape

Drafting tape is similar to masking tape, but it lifts off more easily. It is used to tape paper to the drawing surface and to tape tracing paper over finished drawings.

Plastic Templates

Templates are pieces of plastic with openings shaped to represent the symbols used in architectural drawing. They make it easy to place furniture, kitchen equipment, and bathroom fixtures on a plan. Templates come in several scales, so be sure to purchase ¼″ scale. Also available are ⅛″ lettering guides.

Drawings of furniture, equipment, and fixture symbols are provided in this book (p. 97). These can be traced or photocopied, colored, and cut out. When planning room arrangements, you can move these pieces around on your drawing. After you have decided on an arrangement, you can use the templates to draw each item into position.

Planning for People

1

Interior design magazines, on occasion, show photographs of rooms so exotic and unusual that the reader is left wondering what type of person could inhabit such a space. These rooms often were designed as model rooms in department stores and were intentionally planned as a form of entertainment and spectacle. Model rooms can serve as inspiration for creative problem solving and are often a good opportunity to view the latest furniture and materials on the market. However, few people would be comfortable having such designs in their own homes.

Living space must be planned with people in mind, and people are most at home in surroundings that reflect their own life styles and tastes. The successful interior design is thus one that has been a participatory process. This means that, if you are designing your own home, you should take into account the needs, desires, preferences, and tastes of those who will share it with you. If, on the other hand, you are designing for clients, you must help your clients to articulate their needs and preferences and, with the clients, shape those preferences into a home that works for them.

The designer's first task, then, is to assemble and analyze information about the people who are to live in the home. Some architects and interior designers gather this information through informal discussions with their clients. Others prefer to use a written survey as a starting point. The written survey has several advantages. In a professional situation it allows the client and the client's family to explore their ideas about the home with some direction but in the absence of the designer. Even if you are designing for yourself, the survey provides a structured method of accumulating information from other members of your household. It may even help you to clarify your own ideas.

Two of the projects in this section call for the filling out of a detailed Profile Questionnaire—one for yourself and your household, another for a quite different household. This exercise is meant to open up your thinking about the various possibilities available in interior design and the ways in which they can be shaped for special needs.

A third project involves the assembly of a design notebook, which will be kept throughout this projects manual. The design notebook is a wonderful, growing resource for ideas, samples, sketches—all the raw materials that go into interior design.

Project 1
Profile Questionnaire for Your Own Household

Problem

To discover the range of needs and desires that affect design decisions in your own home, fill out the Profile Questionnaire as it pertains to your own living situation, tastes, personality, and life style.

Procedure

1. Make several photocopies of the Profile Questionnaire on pages 87 to 92—one for each member of your household who would participate in design decisions. (You may want to make several extra copies for use in Project 2.)

2. Assume you are about to have your home designed by a professional, and that your answers to the questionnaire will determine the results of that design.

3. Fill out one questionnaire for yourself, and ask each member of your household to fill out a copy independently, without consulting the others.

4. Answer the questions fully and honestly. You will be using the results as a basis for other projects in this manual.

5. If you are living in a dormitory, you may prefer to fill out the questionnaire as it relates to your family home. You are also free to use the dormitory room for your profile.

6. Analyze all the questionnaires for your household, and write a short paper discussing the varying needs and preferences. Which ones are in harmony? Which are in conflict? How could the conflicts be resolved?

Project 2
Profile Questionnaire for a Different Household

Problem

To discover the range of needs and desires of people with different life styles, find a household that is quite different from your own. If possible, choose a family who will be able to cooperate with your study throughout the course.

Procedure

1. Choose a household that is different from your own in terms of number of household members, occupations, hobbies, pets, income level, life style, tastes, and so forth. (For example, perhaps your household is composed of three university students with part-time jobs, whose interests are primarily books, music, and art. You may want to choose for this exercise a household with a combined income of $40,000, consisting of a husband and wife with three elementary school-age children, whose interests are mainly camping and sports.)

2. Ask the family to assume that they are about to have their home designed by a professional and that filling out the questionnaire is the first step in the design process.

3. Make a copy of the questionnaire for each member of the household who would participate in making design decisions. Ask each member to complete the form without consulting other members.

4. Ask them to answer the questions fully and honestly. You will be using the results of the questionnaire as the basis for other projects in this workbook.

5. Analyze all the questionnaires filled out by this household, and write a short paper discussing the varying needs and preferences. Which are in harmony? Which are in conflict? How could the conflicts be resolved?

Project 3
A Design Notebook

Problem

Start a design notebook in which you will keep your completed and ongoing projects, samples, sketches, and notes.

Procedure

1. Section off a 3-ring loose-leaf notebook with twenty dividers. There should be one divider for each section in this manual, with extra dividers for categories you might like to add. Your 3-hole paper should be solid white and heavy enough to support clippings glued on.
2. Make labels for each section to correspond to the sections in this manual, such as "Planning for People," "Planning for Space," "Elements of Design," and so forth.
3. Keep all written projects, such as the filled-out profile questionnaires and your papers analyzing them, in the notebook.
4. Keep ongoing projects in the notebook. An example of an ongoing project would be collecting newspaper and magazine clippings that illustrate a particular design style.

Consider

This notebook has two purposes: first, to organize written projects so that they can be referred to easily; second, to encourage you, in ongoing projects, to search for and collect illustrations and samples of good design. The more you look, the more sensitive and selective you will become.

Planning for Space

2

After having assembled and analyzed information about the household members, the designer's next task is to translate the space the household occupies into some sort of physical reality. The space itself cannot be drawn, but the outlines that shape the space can be. The three basic types of drawings to indicate space in the home are: the *schematic diagram*, the *floor plan* (which includes the *rough sketch*), and the *elevation*.

A schematic diagram is a freehand drawing of circular or free-form shapes. It roughly outlines different space uses. In their proportion to each other, the shapes show the relative size and importance of each area and of the activities that will take place there. The diagram also establishes relationships among various spaces by means of connecting lines. Arrows on the diagram signify openings as well as circulation paths. When a home is being built, the schematic diagram is used to plot out what types of areas are needed and how these areas will interrelate. In an existing space, the locations of a kitchen and bathrooms will somewhat dictate the arrangement of space, but analysis with a schematic diagram still can be helpful.

The floor plan is nothing more than a precise, accurate interpretation of the schematic diagram. The floor plan begins when the designer makes a rough sketch of the room, takes measurements, and records the measurements on the sketch.

A rough sketch is, and should be, just that—rough. In the case of a professional designer, time is a factor, because the sketch is made at the client's home. The sketch and measurements must be made as efficiently as possible.

From the rough sketch, the designer makes the floor plan, this time with exact dimensions and relationships. This is a basic tool for planning the interior design of a room or home.

If the ceiling were taken off your room and you were floating high above it, what you would see would be quite similar to the floor plan. As you floated down closer to the room, it would seem as though you were looking down into a box. Imagine that the box were slit at each corner and all the sides were pressed down flat. You would then be looking at a floor plan and four elevations. An elevation is a two-dimensional side view, showing how space is organized vertically.

The floor plan and the elevation are drawn as if they were perpendicular to the observer's line of sight. No perspective is used. All details are drawn parallel to the drawing surface. All forms retain their true size (to scale) proportions.

Remember:

- A floor plan illustrates width and depth.
- An elevation illustrates height and width.

Architects and interior designers use conventional symbols to indicate fixtures, furnishings, electrical outlets, switches, doors, and so forth. A chart of the most common symbols appears on pages 93 – 95.

Project 4
Drawing a Schematic Diagram
of Your Own Home

Problem

To analyze how the spaces in your home are being used and how they interrelate by drawing a schematic diagram of your home.

Procedure

1. Draw each area in your home as a rough circular or free-form shape. In their proportion to each other, the shapes should show the relative size and importance of each area and of the activities that will take place there.

2. Draw connecting lines between the shapes to indicate how the areas connect.

3. Refer back to the profile questionnaire you completed for Project 1. Do the areas in your schematic diagram work for the needs and preferences of your household? (For instance, your schematic diagram may show no study areas, and yet on your questionnaire you stated that you needed space for quiet study at home.)

4. How could you alter the areas in your schematic diagram so that they would work better for you? Notice the two schematic diagrams below. Both show the same L-shape apartment. The one at left illustrates traditional use of the areas. The one at right is an alternative plan, in which the living room now doubles as a sleeping area and the bed alcove has become a work area.

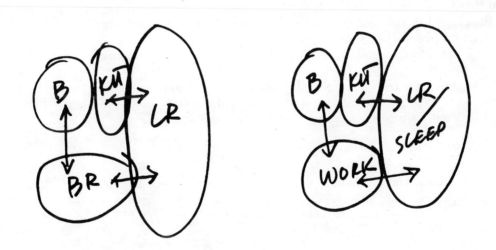

①. 1ˢᵗ step in designing a new home.
② 1ˢᵗ step in remodeling:
  ⓐ diagram as house is now.
  ⓑ diagram with new changes.

Project 5
Drawing a Rough Sketch of Your Own Bedroom

Problem

To draw a rough sketch of your bedroom, in preparation for drawing the floor plan.

Procedure

1. Look at the room you are about to draw.

2. Make a rather large sketch of the room on 3-hole paper, putting in the juts and jags, but not worrying about proportions.

3. Along the room outline mark the locations of doors, windows, and closets.

4. Start measuring in a corner, and measure to the first opening or turn in the wall—door opening, a window opening, a corner, and so forth. Measure to the opening, not to the window or door frame. Put these measurements on your sketch as you go along. Continue until you reach the corner where you started.

5. Measure the overall length and width of the room.

6. Check your measurements in step 4, by adding up the separate measurements for each wall. Do they correspond to the measurement of the whole wall taken in step 5?

7. Indicate whether the doors open into or away from the room and at which side the hinges are placed.

8. Check to see that you have not forgotten to include other permanent fixtures, such as radiators or a fireplace.

9. If there is a closet, measure its depth and width. Measure the depth of any shelves. Note whether the closet has a clothes rod. Note if the closet has a door and what type it is. Refer to the symbols chart on pages 93–94 for closet symbols.

10. Refer again to the symbols chart, and indicate where the electrical outlets, fixtures, and switches are placed.

11. Mark down the ceiling height, the height of doors and windows, the distance between floor and window sills, and the height of other permanent fixtures in the room. These measurements will be used for projects that involve drawing elevations.

Consider

As you look and draw, you are judging spatial relationships. Your first rough sketches will probably be quite lopsided. This is perfectly all right, because they are supposed to be rough. With practice, you will find that the proportions in your sketch will relate closely to the actual room proportions.

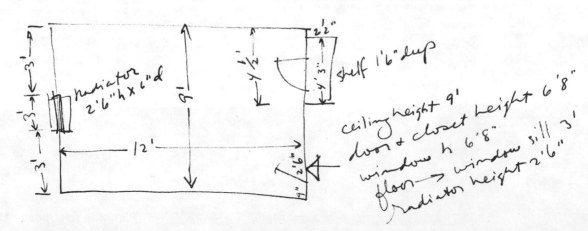

Project 6
Drawing a Detailed Floor Plan of Your Own Bedroom

Problem

To draw a detailed floor plan of your bedroom based on the rough sketch made in Project 5.

Procedure

1. Tape a piece of ¼″, 8½ × 11″ graph paper onto your drawing surface.

2. Using the scale ¼″ = 1′, mark off the large measurements of the room. Work with a hard pencil, employing light pressure. The result is the inside wall of the room.

3. Draw another set of lines outside the first to show the thickness of the walls. One-half of a square would indicate a 6″ wall. This is the usual way to represent a load-bearing wall. Walls that are not load-bearing—that is, those that do not support the structure of the building—are represented with thinner walls.

4. Mark the location and size of openings on your plan—the windows, closets and doors.

5. Erase the wall lines between the openings of the closets and doors.

6. To indicate a window, draw a third line between the inner and outer wall lines (see example).

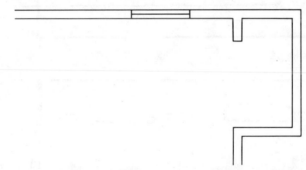

7. If the openings to the room and the closet have doors, check the door symbols on the symbols chart (p. 93). Draw in the appropriate symbols for the doors in your room.

8. If your room has a closet, check the closet symbols on the symbols chart (p. 93), and draw in the appropriate one. Note that a dotted line indicates a shelf or hanging cabinet. A clothes rod is shown by two closely spaced parallel lines.

9. Using a softer pencil, shade the area that represents wall thickness.

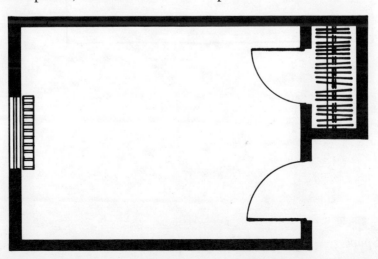

10. Use an Artgum eraser to clean up any areas that have become smudged and gray.

11. If your instructor wants floor plans on drawing paper or illustration board, transfer your plan using the architect's scale to measure and the T-square and triangle to draw.

12. Mount the detailed floor plan on a sheet of illustration board.

13. Place a piece of tracing paper over the plan to protect it. Fasten the tracing paper with two pieces of tape at the top edge so the tracing paper can be lifted.

Consider

Keep the points of your pencils sharp by rubbing them frequently on sandpaper and by rotating them as you draw. If you find that your hand is smearing the drawing, try resting your hand on a piece of tracing paper to protect your work.

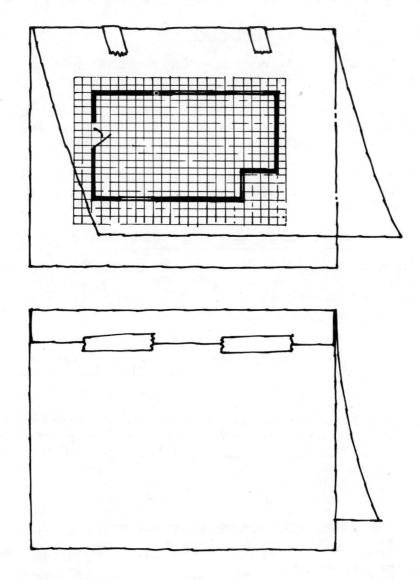

Project 7
Drawing a Detailed Floor Plan and Elevations of Your Bedroom

Problem

To draw the complete floor plan and four side-wall elevations of your own bedroom, based on the floor plan made in Project 6.

Procedure

1. Take a piece of ¼" graph paper large enough to accommodate a floor plan and four elevations. If your room is 9 x 12' or smaller and has a standard 8' or 9' ceiling, a sheet of paper 8½ x 11" will do. If the room is larger or has a high ceiling, use 11½ x 14" graph paper.

2. Tape the graph paper to your drawing surface.

3. Using the scale ¼" = 1', and working with a hard pencil, copy the detailed floor plan of your bedroom (see Project 6) onto the center of the graph paper. Before you draw in the final position of the lines, check to make sure there is enough room on all four sides for the ceiling height.

4. If there is a closet in the room, include the wall the closet is on and the closet door, but do not add the depth of the closet.

5. Refer back to the height measurements you made on the rough sketch (Project 5). Draw the outline for each of the four walls. Do not let the shaded walls around the floor plan confuse you. They will stand between the floor and the walls even though this is not true as you look at your room. The width of the walls should be drawn to correspond to the interior measurements of the room. When measuring the height of the walls, measure up from the outside edge of the shaded walls (see example).

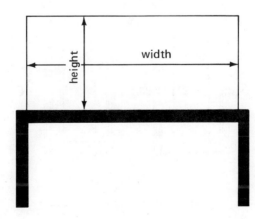

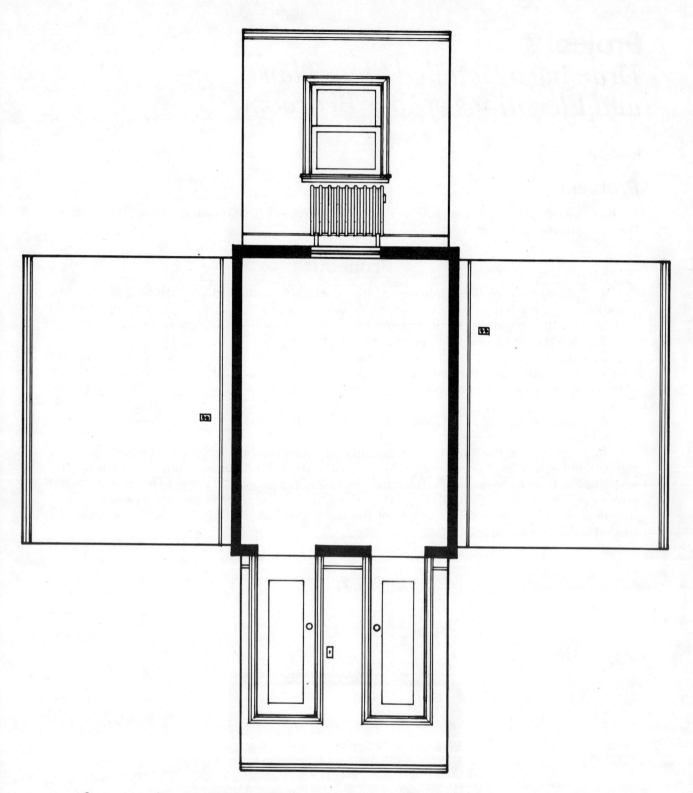

6. Again referring to the height measurements on the rough sketch, draw in the doors, windows, radiators, fireplace, and any other *permanent* fixtures that you see as you look at the wall. Do not include furnishings.

7. Use the Artgum eraser to clean up any areas that have become smudged and gray.

8. If your instructor prefers, transfer your plan and elevations to drawing paper or illustration board using the architect's scale, T-square, and triangle.

9. Mount the drawings on illustration board.

10. Place a piece of tracing paper over the drawings to protect them.

Project 8
Traffic Paths within Your Own Bedroom

Problem

To determine the efficiency of traffic patterns within your bedroom, based on the detailed floor plan.

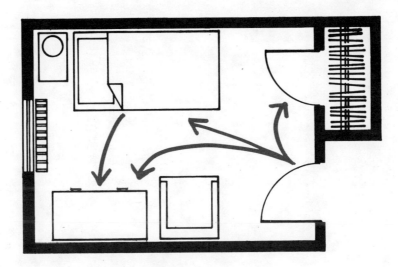

Procedure

1. Tape a sheet of tracing paper over the floor plan for your bedroom (Project 6).
2. Using pencil, draw in the furniture in your room in approximate scale. You can either work with a plastic furniture template or trace the furniture symbols in the symbols chart (pp. 97–98).
3. With a felt-tip pen, draw in the traffic paths from door to bed, door to closet, chest of drawers to closet, door to chest of drawers, and any other common paths.

Consider

Does the furniture arrangement aid or obstruct circulation within the room? If it obstructs, how could this be corrected?

Elements of Design

3

Certain *elements* are common to all areas of design, including interior design. These are: line, shape, form, space, texture, light, and color. You should learn to understand these elements as they operate in the design of a home. While you may not list them consciously when you plan a design. an awareness of the elements will help you to evaluate your designs and perhaps to correct problems that may arise. For example, you may have conceived a design, either on paper or in an actual room, that somehow does not "work," that is not so successful as you would like. An analysis of the design elements might show that the space in the design has not been handled well, or that there is an absence of line to provide definition of space.

This section contains projects dealing with line, shape, space, and texture. Light and color, being so vital to interior design, are dealt with individually in Sections 5 and 6.

Project 9
Analysis of Lines in Interior Design

Problem

To draw and analyze the lines on one wall of your home.

Procedure

1. Choose one wall of your home that will be suitable for drawing an elevation. You may use one of the bedroom elevations made in Project 7, if you wish. However, for this project the wall selected should have several pieces of furniture, some enrichment on the walls (paintings, posters, photographs, and so on), and at least one permanent fixture, such as a door or window. See the example shown here.

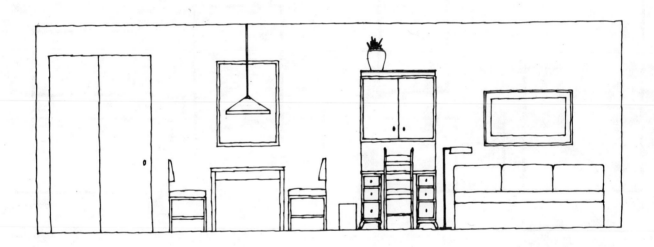

2. Tape a piece of ¼″, 8½ x 11″ graph paper onto your drawing surface.
3. Using the scale ½″ = 1′ (the half-inch scale works better for this project), mark off the height and width of the wall. Work with a medium-soft pencil, so that the lines are fairly dark.
4. Take height and width measurements of all the permanent fixtures on the wall—doors, windows, fireplace, radiator, moldings, built-in bookcases, and so on.
5. Draw the permanent fixtures onto your elevation.

6. Roughly sketch in the furnishings on the wall. Do not worry about perspective or projection into the room. Simply draw the furnishings as though you were looking at them straight on, as though they were flat, two-dimensional cutouts. Include all artwork, plants, bookshelves, lamps, and other objects of enrichment.

7. Tape a piece of tracing paper over your finished elevation.

8. With a felt-tip pen or marker, trace the outside lines of the furnishings and fixtures (see example).

9. Remove the tracing paper from the elevation.

10. Analyze the lines on your tracing in terms of the questions listed below.

Consider

Are the lines on your tracing predominantly horizontal, vertical, or diagonal?
Are the lines predominantly straight or curved?
Do the lines flow into one another, or are there large spaces between them?
Are the lines long and smooth, or are there many changes of direction?
Which of the following adjectives *best* describes the effect of the lines in your tracing: restful, energetic, cheerful, heavy, light, stable?

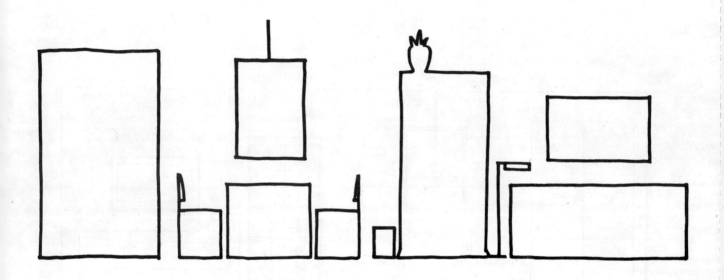

Step one — Outline shapes.
Step two — Fill in shapes.
Step three — Line up elevations ▭▭▭▭
     ① Continuity of forms
     ② Variation for interest
     ③ Line Movement

Project 10
Analysis of Shapes in Interior Design

Problem

To draw and analyze the shapes on one wall of your home.

Procedure

1. Tape a clean piece of tracing paper over the elevation made for Project 9.
2. With a broad felt-tip pen or marker, shade in the *shapes* of furnishings, fixtures, and enrichment on the wall (see example).

3. Remove the tracing paper from the elevation.
4. Analyze the shapes on your tracing in terms of the questions listed below.

Consider

Are the shapes predominantly geometric or free-form?
If geometric, are the shapes predominantly rectangular, circular, or angular?
Is there a balance between rectilinear and curved shapes?
Do the shapes overlap, or are there always spaces between them?
Which of the following adjectives *best* describes the effect of
the shapes in your tracing: restful, energetic, cheerful, heavy, light, stable?

Project 11
Study of Space Modulation through Color and Pattern

Problem

To discover some of the ways in which color, value, and pattern on walls, ceiling, and floor can modulate the space in a room.

Procedure

1. Make at least five photocopies of the outline drawing on this page.

2. Try at least five of the variations listed below. In each instance, analyze the results to determine whether the room seems smaller, larger, shorter, longer, taller.

a. Using a dark-value felt-tip pen or watercolor, shade the entire ceiling, leaving the walls and floor white.

b. Using a dark-value felt-tip pen or watercolor, shade the entire floor area, leaving the walls and ceiling white.

c. Using a dark-value felt-tip pen or watercolor, shade the two side walls, leaving the end wall, floor, and ceiling white.

d. Using a dark-value felt-tip pen or watercolor, shade the end wall and the floor, leaving the side walls and ceiling white.

e. Using a medium-value felt-tip pen, draw a rough lattice-pattern wallpaper design on all three walls, leaving the floor and ceiling white.

f. Find an advertisement for tile flooring in a magazine, and cut out a section the size of the floor in the drawing. Paste the cutout in position.

g. Using a dark-value felt-tip pen, draw a floral wallpaper pattern on the end wall only, leaving the side walls white. With the felt-tip pen or watercolor, shade the floor a dark value.

h. Using watercolor, shade all three walls a medium-light value. Shade the floor a dark value. Leave the ceiling white.

Consider

A dark color seems to lower a ceiling. Light-colored ceilings seem higher.

A room that is too long and narrow can be made to appear more square by a dark color or active pattern on the end walls.

A room that is too square can be given definition by a dark color or active pattern on one or two walls.

All light colors and patterns usually make a room look larger.

All dark colors and patterns usually make a room look smaller.

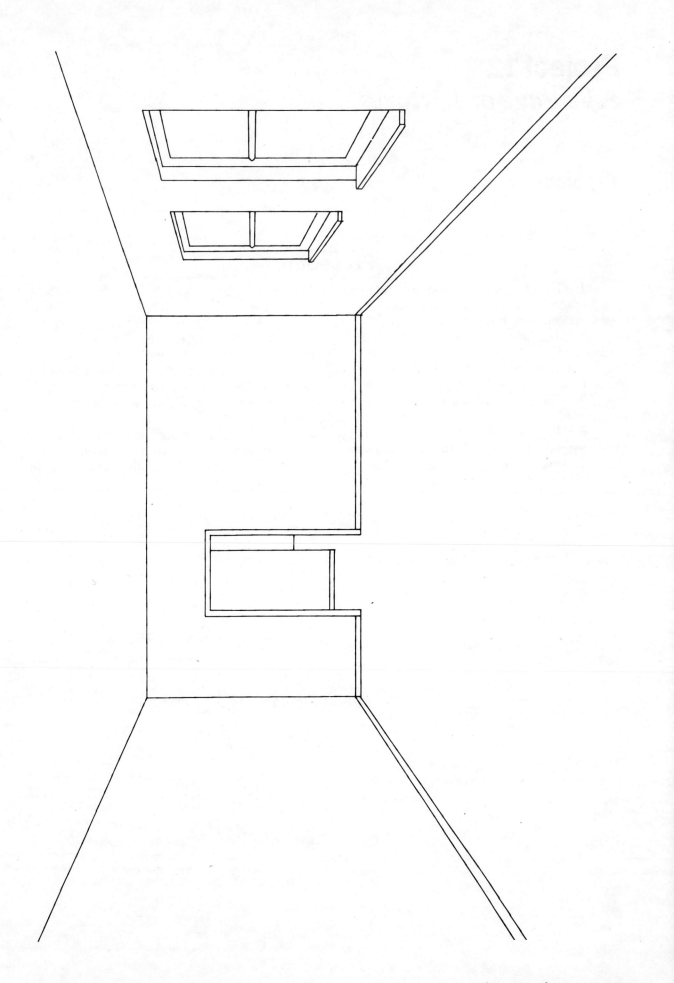

Project 12
A Collage of Textures

Problem

To become familiar with the collage technique and to study the ways in which textures interrelate in interior design.

Procedure

1. Collect scraps of materials that have different textures, from rough to smooth. Include at least one example each of wood, smooth fabric, crinkly fabric, smooth wallpaper, and pile fabric (such as velvet or carpeting).

2. Arrange the scraps of material into a square or rectangular format. Try to achieve a balance of smooth and rough textures. Do not attempt to simulate a room, with carpeting texture at the bottom and smooth fabric where the walls would be. Instead, treat your collage as an art object, and make a pleasing arrangement of textures in relation and proportion to each other.

3. When you have arrived at an arrangement that satisfies you, mount the collage on stiff cardboard. Use staples or glue to attach the scraps to the cardboard.

4. Place the collage on a table, and subject it to a strong light coming from one side, a few inches above the collage. How does the sharp side light change the pattern of textures?

5. Make a photocopy of your collage to eliminate differences of color. Is the relationship of textures still pleasing?

Principles of Design

4

The principles of design are concepts that have evolved to explain how and why certain combinations and relationships of elements please us or perhaps seem unpleasant. The principles that are used to analyze designs are: scale and proportion, balance, rhythm, emphasis, variety, and unity.

These concepts are not rules, but it is important to become familiar with them. One must look at many examples of effective and ineffective design before one is able to sense and apply the principles intuitively. Once the basics have been internalized, the designer can allow the imagination free play and even deliberately violate the so-called principles. This process can be likened to the development of a painter whose work is spontaneous and free, yet grounded in experience.

We have seen that our responses to the elements and principles of design are often emotional and personal, rather than logical. The last project in this section was designed to reveal emotional feelings about living spaces and to allow the imagination free play to design a fantasy home.

Project 13
Using the Principles of Design to Analyze a Room

Problem

To analyze a picture of a living room, using the principles of design as a guide.

Procedure

1. Look through magazines until you find a color photograph of a living room that appeals to you. The picture should be a wide-angle view of the room, rather than just one area.

2. Cut out the picture, and paste it to a piece of 3-hole paper. If it does not fit, paste it to a large piece of paper or illustration board.

3. Write a brief analysis of the room, using the principles of design as a guide.

Consider

Scale—Is the scale of the furniture appropriate for the architectural scale? Is there consistency of scale among the different pieces of furniture? Is the room compatible with human scale?

Proportion—Look at one of the large pieces of furniture. Has it been designed so that its parts are in proportion to the whole?

Balance—Give examples of how visual weights have been balanced in the room. Can you find examples of symmetrical, asymmetrical, and radial balance in the room?

Rhythm—Can you find examples of repeated rhythms in the room?

Emphasis—Using a four-point scale of importance, which areas or objects in the room would you consider to be: emphatic? dominant? subdominant? subordinate?

Unity—How has unity been achieved in the room?

Variety—Give a few examples of variety in the room.

Project 14
Fabrics Illustrating Types of Rhythm

Problem

To collect and analyze fabric swatches that illustrate the different types of rhythm.

Procedure

1. Collect swatches (or pictures) of fabrics that demonstrate each of four kinds of rhythm: repetition, alternation, progression, and contrast.

2. Mount the swatches on a piece of 3-hole paper in your notebook, and label them according to the type of rhythm each exemplifies.

3. Bring the swatches to class to compare and discuss.

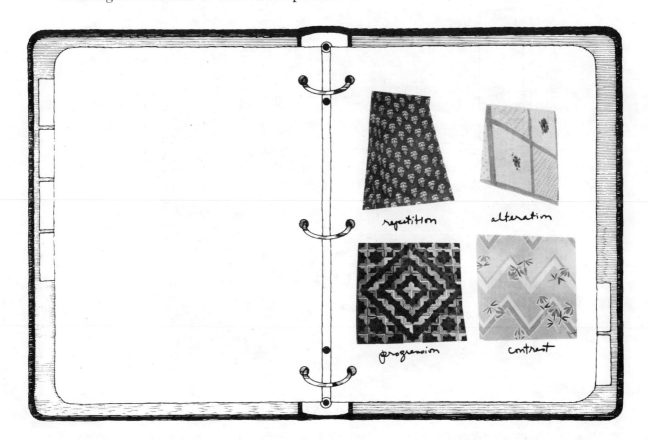

Consider

How could each of these types of rhythm be adapted to other aspects of interior design, such as furnishings or an entire room?

Project 15
A Magazine Paste-Up Using the Principles of Design

Problem

To do a paste-up of an interior using magazine clippings of various furnishings, guided by the principles of design.

Procedure

1. Trace or photocopy the room outline on this page; or, if you prefer, draw it to a larger scale.

2. Cut out from magazines many different examples of furnishings, accessories, fabrics, wall coverings, carpets, and rugs. Get a good assortment, aiming for roughly the same scale overall. Do not try for exact scale, and do not worry too much about perspective.

3. Try different arrangements on your outline until you find one that satisfies you.

4. Paste the cutouts onto your outline drawing.

5. If you wish, you may sketch in additional items to pull the arrangement together.

6. Mount the paste-up on a piece of illustration board.

7. Analyze your paste-up in terms of the principles of design: scale, proportion, balance, rhythm, emphasis, variety, and unity.

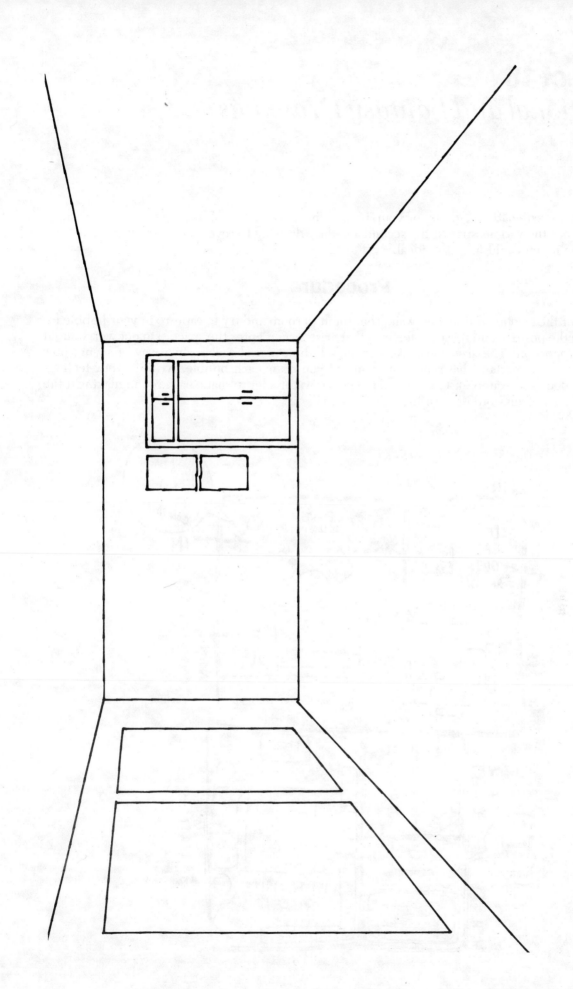

Project 16
Emotional and Fantasy Drawings

Problem

To make two schematic diagrams of your home, the first to reveal any negative and positive feelings about the various spaces, the second a fantasy drawing to reveal how you would like your home to be if you could have the ideal.

Procedure

1. For the *emotional* drawing, walk from room to room and try to capture in your bubble for each room the positive and negative feelings that arise as you enter the space. Do not worry about scale or proportion. The size you make a room's bubble may be your own way of saying how important or unimportant that room is to you. As you draw each bubble, write in your feelings about the room (see example). Use colored pencils or watercolor to shade each room, making it the color the room "feels" rather than the color it actually is.

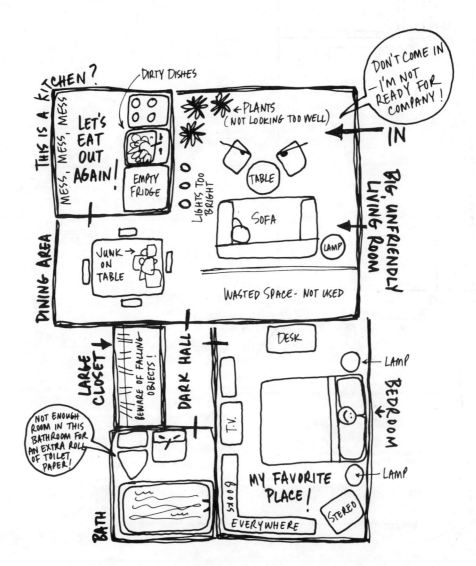

2. For the *fantasy* drawing, do a schematic diagram of your home as you would like it to be if problems of money, space, and all notions of "right" or "wrong" could be eliminated. Again, write in your feelings about each space. Shade each room a color to show what feeling you would like in that room.

3. Compare the two drawings. Were the negative feelings replaced by positive feelings in the fantasy drawing? How impossible is the fantasy drawing? Do problems of space and money prevent you from realizing your fantasy? How could your fantasy become part of your reality? What negative and positive feelings were revealed in the emotional drawing?

Consider

For the professional interior designer, this is a good exercise to use with clients who are willing to do it. The emotional drawing often will reveal feelings about the home that might not come out in an interview. The fantasy drawing can be a starting point for making decisions about the interior design of the home. With some ingenuity, the designer may actually be able to fulfill many of the client's dreams—or at least to come close to them.

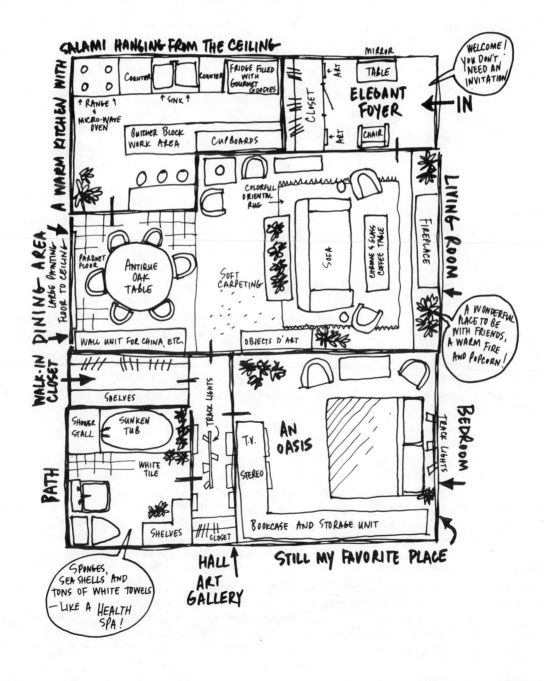

Light

5

The *lighting* for any home must be planned with two things uppermost in mind: the people who will live in the home and the activities that will take place there. Nearly every room in the home needs varied levels of lighting. For example, a kitchen usually will have bright, general lighting, plus more intense, focused lighting over the work areas. At the same time, provisions should be made for lower levels of lighting so that people can pass through the room safely when it is not in active use. Similarly, a living room might serve, at different times, for quiet reading or study and for festive parties. These two kinds of activities have quite different lighting requirements.

In general, there are five categories of lighting that might be appropriate at different times in different areas:

Intimate lighting focuses attention, below eye level, on one small area. It creates an island of space for one or two people and is suitable for talking and relaxing.

Dramatic lighting adds impact to a space by contrasting light and shadow, by drawing special attention to one object or area, or by being an art form in itself. Examples would be lighting a plant from underneath to cast shadows on the wall; directing a ceiling spot on a painting or piece of sculpture; or using a neon bulb as light and art.

Sociable lighting is similar to intimate, but the light covers a larger area. It usually falls on a horizontal plane below eye level. Several intimate areas can create a sociable area. The sociable mood will bring together a small group of people.

Expansive lighting illuminates all areas of a space, creating a sense of spaciousness (perhaps excitement). This type of lighting gives a large or active group an atmosphere in which to move around freely. Direct or indirect lighting is needed on the walls to encourage people to move outward. Other areas should be lit with local lighting to focus attention on specific areas, such as a conversation group or a buffet.

Concentrated lighting is required for reading, close work, or table games. The area bathed in concentrated light should be no more than five times as bright as the darkest part of the room.

The projects in this section have been designed to help you identify the needs of a given household for the various types of lighting, as well as to plan this lighting on paper.

Project 17
Drawing Electrical Symbols

Problem

To position electrical symbols on the floor plan of your own home.

Procedure

1. Make a rough sketch (see Project 5) of your own home, including all permanent fixtures, such as doors, windows, closets, and so forth. If you are living in a dormitory, you may either use your family home for the sketch or take a portion of the dormitory. The section used should include a kitchen and bathroom.

2. Take all the necessary measurements of length, width, and distances between fixtures. Write these measurements on your rough sketch.

3. Working from the rough sketch, draw a detailed floor plan of your home (see Project 7).

4. Refer to the Electrical Symbols Chart on page 95, and draw in all the appropriate symbols on your floor plan. To indicate which switch turns on which light or outlet, draw a curved, dotted line from the switch to the light or outlet.

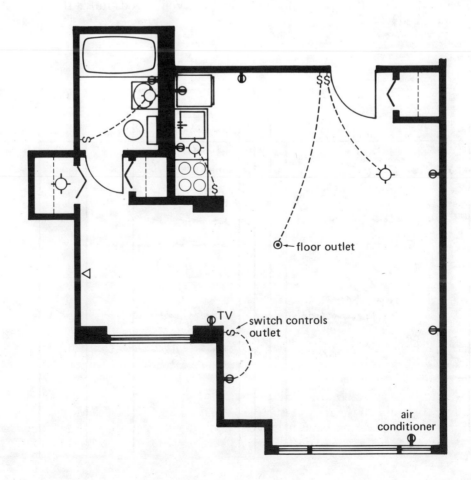

floor outlet

TV

switch controls
outlet

air
conditioner

Project 18
Lighting for Activities

Problem

To determine the ideal lighting for your own home, based on needs and preferences identified in the Profile Questionnaire.

Procedure

1. Refer back to the Profile Questionnaire you completed for Project 1.

2. Based on your answers to the questionnaire, fill out the Lighting for Activities Chart on page 96. (A partially filled-out example is given below.)

3. Begin by listing each room or area in your home, indicating which direction(s) the window(s) face and how the daylight entering these windows is or can be controlled.

4. List the activities that take place in each room. Do not forget those activities that take place infrequently. Perhaps you give a large party only once or twice a year. A successful lighting plan should be flexible enough to adapt to all varieties of activity. Indicate whether the activity takes place mainly during the day or night, or whether it takes place at both times.

5. Decide what mood you would like to set for each activity: intimate, dramatic, sociable, expansive, or concentrated. Check off the kind of lighting you would like to set the mood for each activity.

6. Compare your finished Lighting for Activities Chart with the floor plan of your home in Project 17. Does the present provision for lighting meet your needs fully? If not, how could the situation be improved?

Room or area	Window direction	Daylight controlled by:	Activities	Day	Night	Both	Mood desired	General Direct	General Indirect	Local Task	Local Decorative
Living / Dining Area	East + South	Shades, drapes + awnings	1. talk			✓	Intimate/Social			✓	✓
			2. Read		✓		Concentrated	✓	✓	✓	
			3. TV		✓		concentrated	✓	✓	✓	
			4. Radio/Stereo			✓	Intimate			✓	✓
			5. Piano			✓	concentrated	✓	✓	✓	
			6. Bridge	✓			sociable			✓	✓
			7. Small adult sit-down dinners		✓		sociable/Dramatic		✓	✓	✓
			8. Large adult parties		✓		Expansive/Dramatic	✓	✓	✓	✓

Lighting needed

Project 19
Lighting for Activities— Another Household

Problem

To determine the ideal lighting for a household other than your own, based on the needs and preferences identified in the Profile Questionnaire.

Procedure

1. Refer back to the Profile Questionnaire for a household other than your own that was completed for Project 2.

2. Based on the information in the questionnaire, fill out the Lighting for Activities Chart on page 96. If you wish, you may have one or more members of that household fill out the chart. If you fill out the chart yourself, take the attitude of a professional designer working for a client. There should be sufficient information in the questionnaire for you to complete the Lighting for Activities Chart.

3. Compare the finished Lighting for Activities Chart with the situation that presently applies in that household. Does the present provision for lighting meet this family's needs? If not, how could the situation be improved?

Color

6

To describe any color with reasonable precision, at least three terms are needed: *hue*, the name of a color; *value*, the lightness or darkness of a color; and *intensity* or *chroma*, the degree of purity or grayness.

The simplest and most familiar color theory is based on the concept that there are three basic, or *primary* colors—red, blue, and yellow—that cannot be produced by mixing other colors. However, mixtures of these primary colors will create almost every other color.

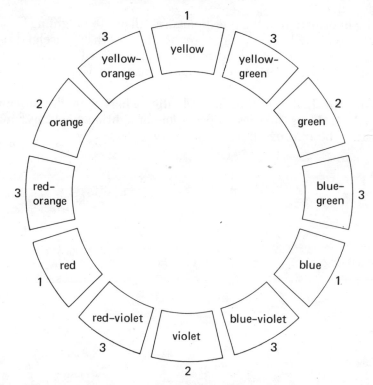

When natural light is passed through a prism, it separates into bands of violet, blue, green, yellow, orange, and red. If these hues are bent into a circle and intermediate hues placed between them, the result is a standard color wheel. In the color wheel shown on this page, the *primary* hues are labeled *1*. *Secondary* hues, which are labeled *2*, result from a combination of two primary hues, as for example yellow mixed with blue will produce green. *Tertiary* hues, labeled *3*, are the result of combining a secondary hue with a primary hue; for example, yellow mixed with green yields yellow-green.

Complementary hues are those that lie directly opposite one another on the color wheel. When complementary hues are placed next to each other, their effect is heightened; each seems stronger and brighter. This effect is known as *simultaneous contrast*. However, when two complementary colors are mixed together, they *neutralize* each other. The result will be a drab brownish gray.

The projects in this section are planned to demonstrate the effects of hue, value, and intensity in colors.

Project 20
A Color Wheel in Fabric

Problem

To create a color wheel using scraps of fabric that approximate the primary, secondary, and tertiary hues on the wheel.

Procedure

1. Study the color wheel on page 36. Try to find a color reproduction of the same wheel or a similar one.

2. Assemble twelve scraps of fabric—one for each of the colors on the color wheel. You will not be able to match the pure colors exactly, but come as close as you can. Do not restrict yourself to plain fabrics. Prints and stripes often work equally well.

3. Arrange the fabric scraps in a circle according to their proper positions on the color wheel. Paste the fabric scraps onto a piece of illustration board, overlapping them slightly at the edges.

4. Label the colors *1, 2,* and *3* according to whether they are primary, secondary, or tertiary colors.

Consider

The interior designer must have a working knowledge of "pure" color theory. But far more important is a sense of color in "real" objects—fabrics, paints, wallpapers, and so forth. This first exercise in working with colors in fabric will help you to visualize their potential effect in a design.

Project 21
Study of Values and Intensities in a Single Color

Problem

To make a value and intensity scale for one of the primary or secondary colors, working in poster paints or similar color medium.

Procedure

1. Select a color of poster paint (or similar paint) that matches one of the primary or secondary colors on the color wheel. Yellow and purple do not work well for this exercise, but you can select from among red, blue, green, or orange.

2. Have available also poster paints in black and white, as well as the color that is complementary to the one you are using for the scale. For instance, if you choose to work with red, you will also need its complement, green.

3. Working with the blank scale on the next page, put a dab of pure color in each of the two boxes marked "start here."

4. Mix equal amounts of white and black paint together to get a medium gray. Mix a very small amount of the gray into your pure color, and put a dab of the resulting color into the box to the right of the starting point on the upper row. Continue in this fashion across the row, each time mixing a bit more of the gray into your color.

5. For the second intensity scale, mix a very small amount of the complementary color into your pure color, and put a dab of the result into the box to the right of the pure color. Continue across the row, each time adding a little more of the complement to the original color.

6. Returning again to your pure color, mix a very small amount of white only into the color, and put a dab in the box above the starting boxes. Continue upward, each time adding a bit more white.

7. Repeat the process with black below the starting boxes. The box nearest to the starting point should have the least black mixed into the pure color, working down to the most black at the bottom.

8. When your value and intensity scale is complete, put it in your notebook.

Consider

You can lower the intensity of a pure color *either* by adding gray or by adding some of the complementary color. Additions of the complement will probably result in a warmer tone.

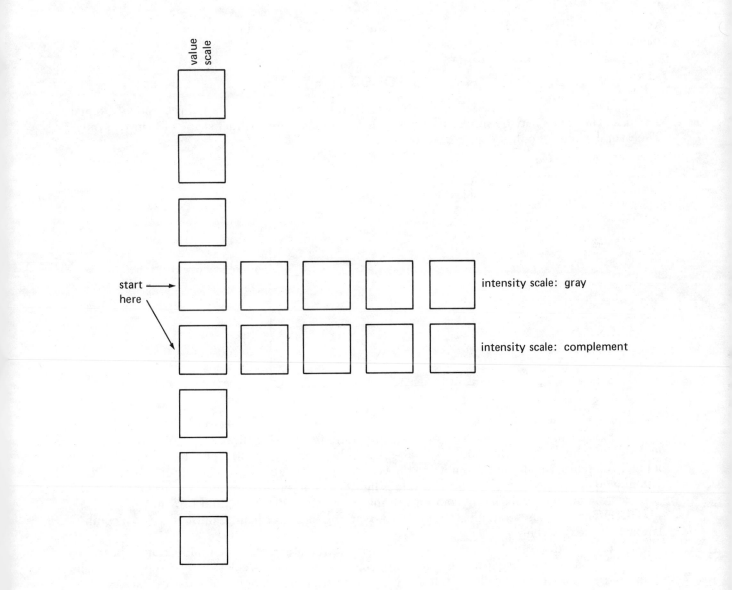

value
scale

start
here

intensity scale: gray

intensity scale: complement

Project 22
Color Harmonies

Problem

To learn to work with color harmonies by planning at least three different harmonies, in poster paint, on abstract shapes.

Procedure

1. Draw an outline shape on illustration board, and divide it into three roughly equal sections. The shape may be similar to the one shown here or any abstract shape of your choosing. The overall shape should be at least 4″ by 4″.

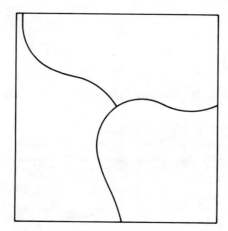

2. Repeat this, so that you have at least three outline shapes on pieces of illustration board.
3. Plan an *analogous* color harmony (see illustration), choosing three colors directly adjacent on the color wheel. Examples would be blue-green, blue, and blue-violet; or red, red-orange, and orange. Remember that you need not use the color at full strength or normal value. You can work with grayed (low intensity) colors or with values lighter or darker than normal. For instance, a red, red-orange, and orange harmony could mean maroon, pale red-orange, and brown.
4. Experiment on scrap illustration board, working in poster paints, until you find a combination that pleases you.
5. Transfer the color harmony you have chosen to the abstract shape on illustration board.
6. Repeat the exercise in a *complementary* color harmony—two colors directly opposite each other on the color wheel (see illustration). When you find a combination that satisfies you, transfer it to your second abstract shape.
7. Again repeat the exercise in a *triad* color harmony—three colors equidistant from each other on the color wheel. Transfer the results to your third abstract shape.
8. If you wish, select another of the color harmonies illustrated here, and repeat the exercise.

Consider

Color harmonies are only guidelines, not rigid rules to follow. Planning with paints or other experimental materials on paper can help you to choose or evaluate the colors for a room, and often will pull the whole design into focus.

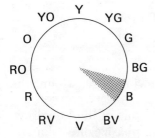

Monochromatic Harmony

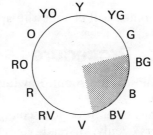

Analogous Harmony

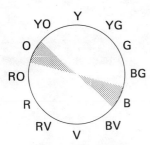

Complementary Harmony

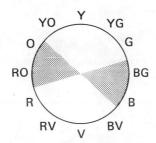

Double-Complementary Harmony

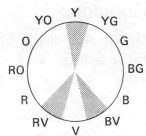

Split-Complementary
Harmony

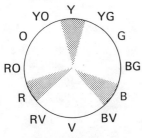

Triad Harmony

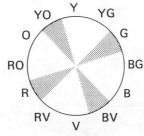

Tetrad Harmony

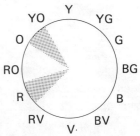

Asymmetric Harmony

Project 23
Color Harmonies in a Room Diagram

Problem

To discover how different color harmonies will change the appearance of a room.

Procedure

1. Make at least three photocopies of the room drawing on the following page. Mount the copies on pieces of illustration board.

2. Working in poster paints, transfer each of your color harmonies to one of the line drawings. You need not distribute the colors evenly. Instead, you may wish to emphasize one color and use either or both of the others as accents.

Consider

How do the different color harmonies affect the appearance of the room?

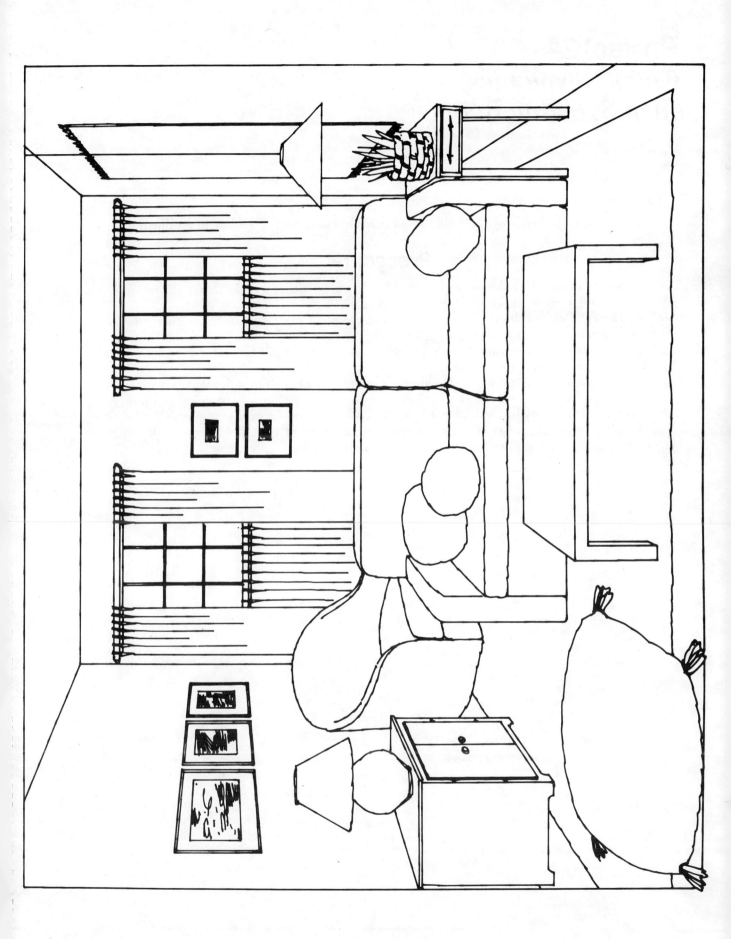

Project 24
Color Harmonies in an Existing Room

Problem

To identify the color harmony operating in an existing room, either real or in an illustration.

Procedure

1. Select a room the colors of which you like. It can be either a real room (perhaps your own bedroom or living room) or an illustration in a magazine.

2. List in a column the principal colors in the room—walls, floor, rug, furniture, draperies, and major accents, such as colorful sofa pillows. Ignore very small spots of color, such as a vase or ashtray or telephone, unless they really attract attention. Use familiar, subjective color names, like turquoise, raspberry, or brown.

3. In a column next to the first column of colors, translate your subjective names into the standard terms from the color wheel (p. 36). Turquoise might be a light value of blue-green, raspberry a low intensity of red-violet, brown a dark-value, low-intensity orange.

4. When you have a list of objective color names, look at the color harmony diagrams on page 41. What is the prevalent color harmony in your room?

The Shell: Floors and Ceilings

7

Floors and ceilings may seem many feet apart, but the design of one constantly influences the other. Just as the ocean's blue is reflected from the sky, so too is a ceiling's color reflected down upon the furniture and flooring. And just as sand reflects more of the sun's light than does grass, so a pale carpet refects more of the ceiling's light than does dark wood flooring. A very high ceiling may need to be weighted down with a dark or bright flooring, while a very low ceiling may require a light flooring to keep the space as open as possible. Ceilings and floors define the three dimensions of our living space—length, width, and height.

Throughout the middle part of this century, floors and ceilings did not get much creative attention from designers. They usually were flat, undifferentiated planes, parallel to each other. Ceilings were most often white, floors either dark wood or solid-color wall-to-wall carpeting.

Recent years have brought a change in the attitude toward these "neutral" surfaces. Architects are designing sloped or varied-height ceilings and changes of floor level into even the most budget-conscious dwellings. The interior designer, too, can exercise great latitude in manipulating floors and ceilings to contribute to the overall design.

The projects in this section are designed to open up your thinking about the various possibilities for floors and ceilings.

Project 25
Raising Floors

Problem

To experiment with different floor levels in a one-room apartment, using a cardboard box as a model.

Procedure

1. Find a cardboard box that, when laid on its side, has the approximate proportions of a one-room apartment. A shoe box often works, but you may want a somewhat larger scale to allow room for maneuvering. If you cannot find a box of the right size and shape, you can make one from heavy cardboard, following the diagram below. (Our imaginary apartment has a separate kitchen and bathroom, so we will ignore those areas.)

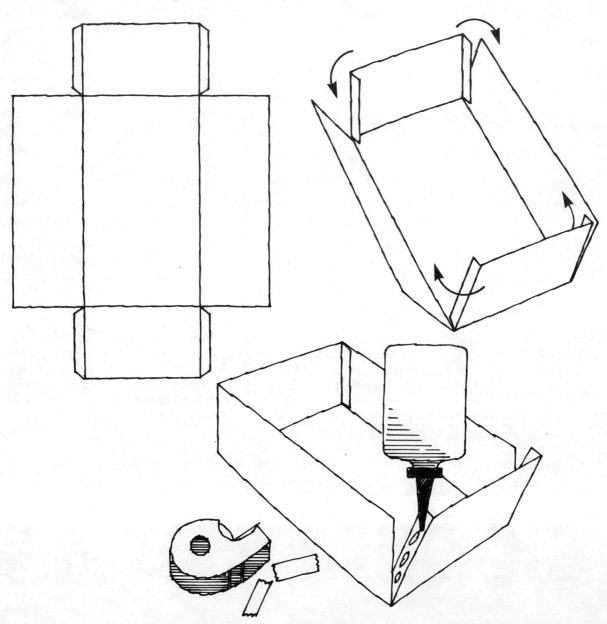

2. Temporarily, draw in two or three windows and a door on the inside walls. As you experiment with levels, you may prefer to place the windows and door elsewhere. Of course, you would not have this luxury if you were working with an actual room, but experimentation is more important than reality in this project.

3. To raise the floor, place smaller boxes of varying heights on the floor of the room box. Again, you can use ready-made boxes or make some from cardboard.

4. Try the boxes on the plan until you have created areas for sleeping, eating, working, and entertaining. Some areas could be used for more than one activity.

5. When you have decided on the final placement of windows and doors, go over their outlines with black magic marker.

6. If you wish, "furnish" your room with dollhouse furniture or cutouts, to see how furnishings work with your new floor levels.

Consider

Building a platform floor or loft is one of the easiest and least expensive structural modifications. Changes in floor level can make a small room seem more defined, a larger one less cavernous. How would you use the space under the new floor levels?

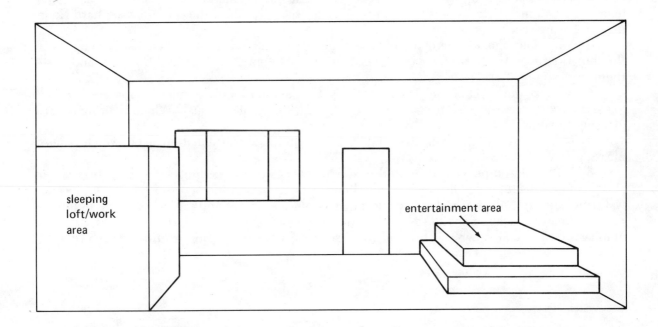

sleeping loft/work area

entertainment area

Project 26
The Cost and Effect of Flooring

Problem

To evaluate four different types of flooring for a given room, considering the cost and design effect of each.

Procedure

1. Imagine that you are selecting new flooring for a family room. You are considering brick, wood parquet tiles, vinyl tile, and nylon wall-to-wall carpeting. The room measures 14 × 17′.

2. Visit a flooring supply store to research the cost and installation charge for each of the four materials. You may have to visit two stores—one for the carpeting, the other for the hard floorings.

3. Make four photocopies of the room outline on page 23. On each, sketch in and color one of the four floorings. If you prefer, you can cut out magazine pictures of these floorings and paste them in position.

4. Analyze the effect of each flooring. Does it make the room look smaller or larger? Does it make the room warm or cold, busy or calm, light or dark, formal or casual? Which flooring is most pleasing to you? Why?

5. Label each drawing with the total cost for material and installation. Now which is most pleasing to you?

6. With colored pencils or diluted poster paints, color the ceilings. If you wish, you can sketch in architectural details, such as moldings or beams. Consider the possibility of fabric or wallpaper on the ceiling. The latter could be cut from magazines and pasted onto the outline.

7. Analyze each room with the ceiling finished. Does it "work" with the floor? Where is the emphasis in the room now? What would you visualize for the walls and furniture in each room?

The Shell: Walls, Windows, and Doors

8

Walls and windows are large elements. Their treatment can be planned either to carry the design or to blend with it. For example, the choice of a strongly patterned wallpaper, a vivid wall color, or a striking drapery fabric will establish the design of a room. On the other hand, a decision to paint the walls white or a pale color, to use neutral fabrics or an unassertive color, will follow from another strong design element, perhaps a brilliant rug.

Despite their size, walls and windows should not necessarily be considered first. They are part of the whole. The designer's efforts must be directed toward the role of walls and windows in affecting mood, character, and spirit—setting the stage for daily living.

Windows and doors have four practical functions. They admit air, light, views, and people, to varying degrees. The designer can control each of these, to the extent needed for a particular room or household, at the same time that purely aesthetic considerations are being planned.

Walls, too, may have very practical functions, in addition to supporting the roof and defining space. Increasingly, walls are being "used" in an active manner. The familiar bookshelves attached to walls have expanded into entire built-in, modular units for every purpose.

Project 27
Checklist for Window Treatments

Problem

To evaluate and redesign the window treatments in a living room, considering the answers to the Profile Questionnaire, and taking into account control of light, air, temperature, views, privacy, as well as aesthetic concerns.

Procedure

Look again at the living room inhabited by the household surveyed in one of the two Profile Questionnaires (Projects 1 and 2)—either your own household or the family other than your own. Reread the completed questionnaire for that household. Assume you are going to completely redesign the window treatments for the living room of that household. Fill out the Checklist for Window Treatments below.

Checklist for Window Treatments

1. In which direction (north, south, and so on) do each of the windows in the room face?
first exposure _____
second exposure _____
third exposure _____

2. Which, if any, of the following undesirable situations applies to the room and its windows?
too-bright morning light _____
hot sun in late afternoon _____
glare _____
room too dark: in summer _____
in winter _____ always _____

3. Does the room have:
cross ventilation _____
windows on one wall only _____
windows on two adjacent walls _____
adequate ventilation _____
inadequate ventilation _____

4. Do any of the following conditions, which might be helped by window treatment, apply to this room?
excessive cold in winter _____
excessive heat in summer _____
excessive dampness _____
both too hot in summer and too cold in winter _____

5. Are the views from the windows:
pleasant _____ unpleasant _____
neutral _____

6. Should the window treatment control the privacy of those inside:
at night _____
during the daytime _____
always _____

7. Is the shape of the windows:
attractive _____ ugly _____
boring _____

8. Are the windows set in the walls:
too high _____ too low _____
about right _____

9. Does this room have any special windows that may need individual treatment?
picture window _____
window wall _____
bay or bow window _____
casement opening inward _____
other _____

10. Should all the windows in the room have the same treatment?
Yes _____ No _____

11. Or does one window call for special treatment different from that of the others?
Yes _____ No _____

12. Are there two or more windows that should be tied together with a common window treatment?
Yes _____ No _____

13. Are there any architectural features (such as a radiator) that affect window treatment?

Yes _____ No _____

14. Will furniture be placed under windows, and, if so, does this affect window treatment?

Yes _____ No _____

15. Will plants be hung at the windows?

Yes _____ No _____

16. Would it be desirable to carry out a fabric pattern, perhaps from upholstery, in a soft window treatment?

Yes _____ No _____

17. In terms of visual effect, should windows be:

emphasized _____ deemphasized _____

neutral _____

Project 28
The Cost and Effect of Window Treatments

Problem

To design two window treatments, one hard and one soft, for each of six kinds of windows.

Procedure

    1. Make an extra photocopy of the six types of windows on the following page, or trace the windows onto another sheet of paper.

    2. Design a soft and a hard treatment for each window.

    3. Sketch the treatments onto each of the windows.

    4. Color your drawings, using poster paints, watercolors, magic markers, or colored pencils.

    5. Decide what are the measurements for each window.

    6. Given the measurements you have chosen, estimate the approximate cost for each treatment by checking prices in catalogues.

Consider

Of the two treatments you have designed for each window, which is the more effective? Which is the more expensive?

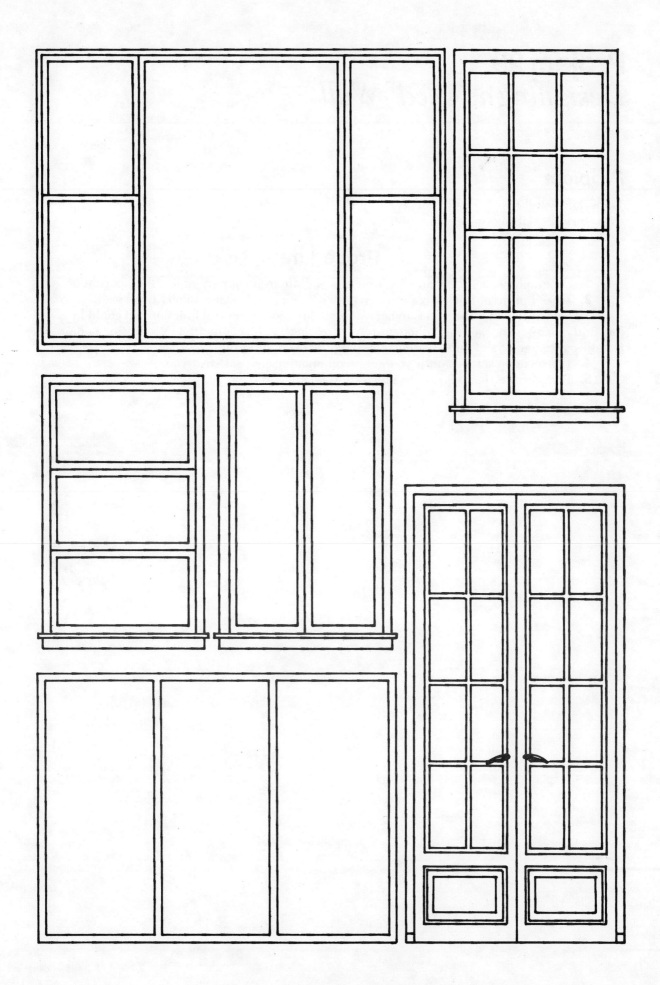

Project 29
Designing a "Used" Wall

Problem

To design a wall that is "used" totally, with built-in bookcases, storage, audio-visual equipment, work surfaces, sitting or sleeping units, and so forth.

Procedure

1. On graph paper, draw an elevation of a wall in an imaginery one-room apartment.
2. Tape a piece of tracing paper over the elevation, and plan a totally used wall.
3. Decide whether the wall is to have a single function or several functions. It could be a wall for study, carpentry, sewing, photography, dressing, entertainment (TV, music, and/or bar facilities), storage of all kinds, seating, sleeping, or even all of these.
4. Try several sketches until you get a combination that satisfies you.
5. Transfer the final version to illustration board.

Hard Materials

9

The interior decorator is constantly making decisions about materials. It is important that these decisions be made knowledgeably, for one poor choice can ruin an entire room. An example might be the selection of an elegant, fragile coffee table for a family that plans to give the table daily use.

The designer today must understand, at the very least, the characteristics, possibilities, strengths, and limitations—plus the costs—of each material. No single material will serve every purpose. The matching of material to use becomes the designer's task.

It is important, too, to know the history of a material in design. Knowing how a material was used in the past can inspire new and creative applications in the present.

The hard materials are considered to be: wood, masonry (brick, stone, and so forth), ceramics, glass, metal, and rigid plastics. Two projects are provided to encourage flexibility in working with these materials.

Project 30
Relative Costs for Kitchen Countertop Materials

Problem

To compare the costs of a kitchen countertop in each of four different hard materials.

Procedure

1. Assume a kitchen countertop a total of 15′ long, with openings for a double sink and a four-burner cooktop, plus a backsplash all around.

2. Check catalogues and stores for the approximate cost of a complete countertop in each of the following materials: maple butcher block, glazed ceramic tile, marble, melamine plastic (Formica and so on).

Consider

Which of these materials would be the most durable? the least durable?

Which of these materials would require the most care? The least care?

How can you balance cost against durability and ease of maintenance?

How much effect does color choice have on selection of countertop materials?

Project 31
Using Hard Materials
in Formal and Informal Interiors

Problem

To design a "formal" and an "informal" room, in each case using at least one of the following hard materials: wood, masonry, ceramics, glass, metal, plastics.

Procedure

1. Make two copies of the room outline on the following page, either by tracing or by photocopying. Mount the outline on illustration board.

2. Cut from magazine and store catalogues examples of furnishings, accessories, wall coverings, and floor coverings that you would need to arrange two interiors on the room outlines. Find as many examples as you can of wood, masonry, ceramics, glass, metal, and plastics.

3. Design one interior to be "formal," the other "informal" in overall effect. Assemble your cutouts on the room outlines, rearranging them until you find a combination you like. Each room must have at least one example each of the various hard materials. Try to avoid the temptation to satisfy all the requirements with small objects and accessories. For instance, a ceramic weed jar would meet the requirement for ceramics in a room, but a fireplace surrounded with ceramic tiles would be more inventive.

4. Aim for roughly the same scale overall, but do not try to exact scale, and do not worry too much about perspective.

5. You may also sketch in some items to pull the design together.

6. When you have an arrangement that satisfies you, paste the cutouts in position.

Consider

A material in itself is not formal or informal. What matters is the way the material is used, and the overall contribution to the design.

Fabrics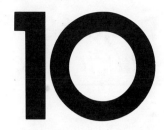

Fabrics humanize our homes. They make us more comfortable, control light coming through windows, give privacy without solid walls, insulate against heat and cold, and absorb noise. Beyond their everday usefulness, however, fabrics have two other important functions. First, they make their own visual and tactile contributions to the home; and, second, they can be strong unifying elements within a room and between rooms.

Fabric is a general term referring to anything manufactured by hand or machine, but it has come to be applied especially to *cloth*. The word *textile* originally referred only to *woven* fabrics. Today, in addition to weaving, fabrics can be made by felting, knitting, or twisting together natural or synthetic fibers and also by fabricating plastics into films, sheets, or molded forms.

Weaving remains the most prevalent method of fabric construction. It consists of the interlacing, by machine or hand, of warp (lengthwise) and filling (crosswise) yarns in some regular pattern. There are three basic categories of weaves.

Plain weave is simply one filling yarn carried over one warp yarn and under the next, alternately across the web. Plain weaves are usually firm and sturdy.

Twill weave has a definite diagonal line or wale on the surface of the fabric. Twills resist soil, wrinkle less, are more flexible, and drape more easily than plain weaves of similar quality.

Satin weave includes yarns that make longer, less regular "floats" on the surface of the fabric. This minimizes the over-and-under texture and may result in a smooth, light-reflecting surface.

Two major variations of these weaves are particularly important in fabrics for interior design.

Pile weaves add to the basic warp and filling a third set of yarns, which protrude from the background as loops. The loops may be cut (velvet) or left uncut (terry cloth).

Jacquard weaves are usually complex pattern weaves produced on a Jacquard loom, which operates something like a computer to create almost any design, from a simple geometric motif to complex, irregular figures. Examples include damasks, brocades, and tapestries.

There is no one fiber perfect for every purpose. Each fiber, whether natural or manufactured, has advantages and disadvantages. Wool and cotton have become favorites for all-around use. This is partly because these natural fibers are familiar to us, but also because new processes can make them resistant to soil and stains, shrinkage and moths, or crushing and wrinkling. Manufactured fibers are growing in popularity, however, for many not only resist but actually repel moisture and soil. Since they are not made from organic substances, they do not attract the insects and fungi that often prey on the natural fibers.

In selecting a fiber or fabric for an interior, the designer should first determine the need and then compare the good and poor qualities of each.

Project 32
Fabric Reference Chart

Problem

As the start of an ongoing project for your notebook, begin a collection of fabric samples.

Procedure

1. Collect at least eight fabric samples, each about 2″ square. Include at least one of each of the three basic weaves: plain, twill, and satin. Also include at least one pile weave and one Jacquard weave. There should be some natural and some synthetic fiber fabrics.

2. Glue the fabric squares, four to a page, on 3-hole white notebook paper.

3. Label each fabric square with as much of the following information as you can find:

name of fabric   care
fiber content   durability
type of weave or other construction   potential uses
special finishes

If the squares are being cut from a bolt or sample, most of this information will be available for you to copy into your notebook. Once you have established the name of the fabric and the fiber content, a standard textile reference book will supply the rest of the information.

Consider

This is a working collection, which you should expand at every opportunity, so that you can refer to it for inspiration and information.

Project 33:
Material Layout and Presentation

Problem

To plan the fabrics for one living room and prepare a material layout and presentation of this design.

Procedure

1. Refer to the Profile Questionnaires completed in Projects 1 and 2. Plan the fabrics for a living room to be designed for either household—your own or the alternate family. Take into account life styles, ages of household members, color preferences, need for privacy, provision for insulation from temperature and sound, and so forth.

2. Decide upon the fabrics that are to be used for walls, window treatments, upholstery, accessories, and floor covering.

3. Choose ceiling, wall, and floor treatments that complement your fabric selections.

4. On illustration board, prepare a material layout similar to the outline drawing shown here. Use swatches and samples of fabrics in the same proportions that they will appear in the room. Arrange the samples so that the ceiling treatment is at the very top, the flooring treatment at the very bottom, and the fabrics in roughly the positions they would occupy in the room. For example, a blue fabric that is used on sofa pillows only should appear as a small piece of blue on the larger sofa fabric.

5. Add ceiling, wall, and floor treatments by sketching, coloring, or attaching paint chips and wood samples. If you paint in the colors, and use color pictures of wood intended for paneling or flooring, you will get a better idea of the overall design effect.

6. On a separate sheet to be attached to the illustration board, list the fabrics, colors, and other elements included.

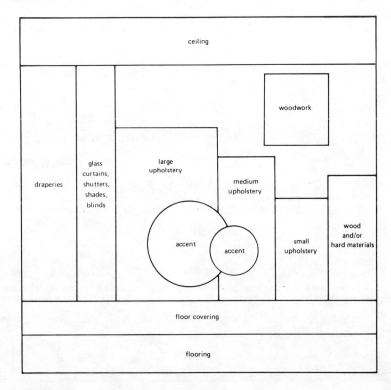

Project 34
Fabrics as a Unifying Element

Problem

To unify a room by means of fabrics on walls, windows, furniture, and so forth.

Procedure

1. Trace or copy the line drawing on the next page; or copy these instructions, and pull the page from the manual. Mount the line drawing on illustration board.

2. Choose a fabric, either plain-colored or patterned, that you will use to unify the room visually. Or, choose two coordinated fabrics.

3. Work with paints, colored pencils, cutouts from magazines, or samples of actual fabric. Paste or paint the fabrics onto the room outline in the areas of your choice, keeping in mind that your goal is to unify (without overwhelming).

4. You may choose to apply the fabric to: walls; floor; ceiling; furniture; windows—any or all of these. You can cover the windows entirely, or make individual window treatments for each.

5. If you wish, sketch in accessories and other elements in the room.

Consider

Fabrics offer one of the easiest and least expensive ways to pull a design together.

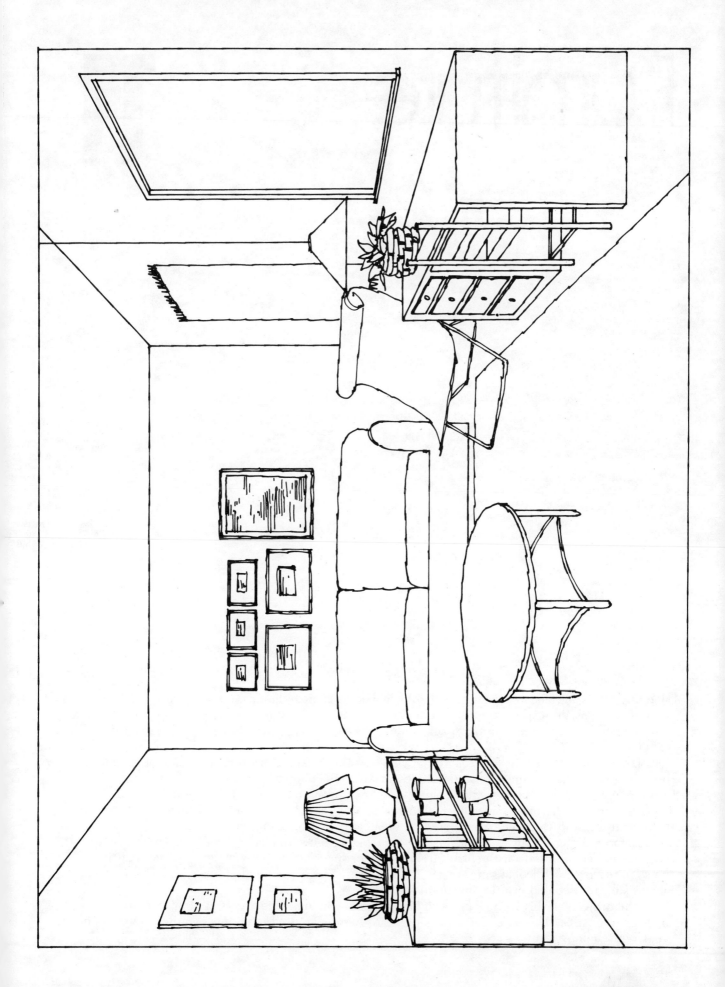

Furniture 11

Furniture should make our spaces "livable." It should add to our comfort while we are eating, sleeping, working, and relaxing, and should make our lives function more smoothly. Furniture should serve as the expression of our personal tastes and, by the design of each piece and the arrangement of all pieces within a space, should define the type of living we expect the space to foster.

Unfortunately, reality is often the reverse of this ideal. Furniture that has been found, inherited, or bought impulsively sometimes makes our living spaces anything but livable. The same people who demand a work-efficient office will often never consider the need for making their homes life-efficient. Uncomfortable, unattractive, and poorly arranged furniture becomes familiar to us, and we forget what potential for beauty and function our spaces hold.

Before purchasing furniture, it is necessary to acquire two things: a sense of one's own taste or that of one's clients; and a list of furniture needed for specific functions. A sense of one's taste can be acquired by much looking in magazines and stores. The list of needed furnishings comes from analysis of the detailed profile questionnaire.

The projects in this section are designed to make you look objectively at your own functional needs and desires. This objective knowledge can then be applied to clients or other members of your household.

Project 35
Designing a Desk or Study Area

Problem

To become familiar with furniture needs by designing your own desk and/or study area, to be built to your order or to be assembled with available components.

Procedure

1. List the elements you would like to have included in an *ideal* work or study area. These should include such items as: writing surface, drawing surface, space for typewriter, storage for supplies, lighting, filing cabinets, display boards, specialized storage, bookcases, whatever you wish. If you sew or practice a craft, you may want to include components for these activities. Audio-visual equipment may or may not be desirable in this area. Remember that it is *your* ideal to be served.

2. Beginning with a rough pencil sketch, design your work/study area, incorporating all the elements you have listed.

3. When you find a combination that satisfies you, complete the design in the medium of your choice—pen and ink, watercolors, magic marker, even collage.

Project 36
Ideal Furniture Heights and Types

Problem

To determine the ideal heights and functions of various furniture types for your body structure and life style.

Procedure

1. Begin filling in the Checklist for Furniture on the next page by inserting your height and weight.

2. If possible, find a swivel chair that adjusts for height. If you cannot obtain such a chair, try sitting in as many straight chairs as are available, until you find the ones most comfortable for the various activities listed below.

3. Find the chair height most comfortable for you when you are studying, writing, and so forth. You should be able to sit fairly upright, without bending excessively over the work surface, but the surface should be an adequate distance from your eyes to prevent eyestrain. Coordinate this height with your ideal work chair height. Enter the height on the checklist.

5. Find the chair height most comfortable for you when you are dining. Your elbows should be slightly below the table surface. Enter the height on the checklist.

6. Consider how many people normally sit down to dinner together in your household. Using the standard sizes for rectangular and round dining tables shown here, determine the best table size for your household (either rectangular or round or both). Enter it on the checklist.

7. Add 6″ to your height as listed on the cheklist. This is the minimum bed length for your height. If you like even more "stretching" room, add 12″ to your height. Working with the standard bed sizes shown here, choose the next longest bed length (75″, 80″, 84″). Enter on the checklist. (Of course, if you *really* like a lot of room, you can certainly choose the largest size. This, then, becomes your ideal.)

8. Determine the ideal width of your bed. A cot or daybed may be adequate for occasional overnights, but for prolonged use, the minimum width for one person is either 36″ or 39″; for two

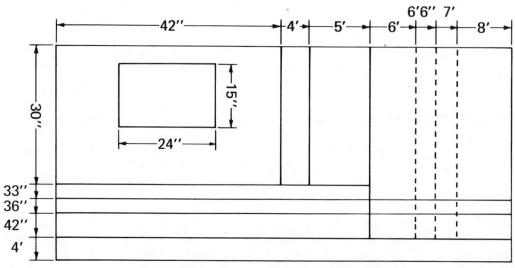

standard sizes for rectangular dining tables

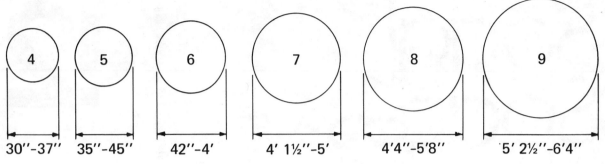

4	5	6	7	8	9
30″–37″	35″–45″	42″–4′	4′ 1½″–5′	4′4″–5′8″	5′ 2½″–6′4″

standard sizes for round dining tables

people, 54″ or 60″. Again, if you enjoy having a great deal of stretching room, there is no reason why you could not choose 76″ for one person. Enter your ideal on the checklist.

9. Consider your favorite position for watching television or listening to music—sitting upright, reclining, lounging, lying down on a sofa, lying on the floor. What piece of furniture would best meet your needs? Enter on the checklist.

Consider

In a household composed of several people, possibly including children, it is difficult to establish the idea for everyone. But once the ideal has been determined, the designer can come as close as possible, making compromises where necessary.

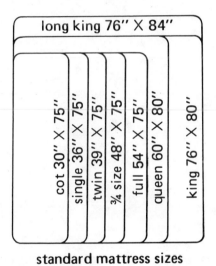

standard mattress sizes

Checklist for Furniture

Height _____ **Weight** _____

Ideal chair height for working _____

Ideal surface height for working _____

Ideal chair height for dining _____

Number of people normally at dinner _____

Ideal table size—rectangular _____

Ideal table size—round _____

Ideal bed length _____

Ideal bed width _____

Favorite position for TV or music _____

Furniture for TV or music _____

Social Spaces

12

The social spaces in any home are the areas where household members gather and where friends are welcomed. They provide an atmosphere for such activities as conversation, games, parties, listening to or making music, eating, and children's play. Most homes throughout history have included such communal gathering places, where the entire household could assemble for recreation, companionship, and often warmth.

The emphasis given to each group activity varies from individual to individual and from household to household. Furthermore, our priorities inevitably change as the years pass. For example, the group space that makes ample provision for children's play will assume a different character when those children are grown. The arrangement of space, then, is a matter of coordinating furnishings with both activities and architecture. Even the tiniest homes benefit from having social spaces demarcated from other zones.

Three projects are presented in this section—all planned to explore solutions to particular design challenges. With the flexibility learned from doing these projects, you should be able to approach almost any design problem.

Project 37

Furniture Arrangement in the Social Spaces of Your Own Home

Problem

To plan and arrange the furnishings in the social spaces of your own home, based on the answers to the Profile Questionnaire.

Procedure

1. Draw a detailed floor plan of the social spaces in your own home. This should include living room, dining area, and family room (if any). If some or all of the kitchen is used as a social space, include this also.

2. Refer to the Profile Questionnaire completed as Project 1. Consider the various activities that will need to be accommodated in the social spaces, either frequently or occasionally.

3. Trace or photocopy the furniture cutouts provided on page 97. Based on those furnishings you have, or would like to have, cut out the items needed to fulfill the functions in your social spaces.

4. Arrange the cutouts on your floor plan. Move them around until you have an arrangement that satisfies you.

5. Consider traffic paths into, out of, and through the room. Is the arrangement still satisfactory? If not, adjust it.

6. Are you allowing sufficient space for traffic and leg room? If not, make the necessary adjustments.

7. Are the conversation areas cozy and inviting? Can all members of a household sit comfortably—in one group or more than one—for a conversation? If not, make the necessary adjustments.

8. Role-play the different situations that might arise in the social spaces. Does the furniture arrangement work for these situations? If not, adjust.

9. When you have decided on a final arrangement, trace the cutouts or use a plastic template to draw the furniture onto the plan.

Project 38
Providing for Various Activities with Modular Seating Units

Problem

To select and arrange furnishings for a room with a built-in audio-visual storage wall at one end, to accommodate three different kinds of activities.

Procedure

1. Make three tracings or photocopies of the floor plan and furniture cutouts on the following page.

2. Assume that your client has asked you to design solutions for three quite different activities. For this room you have chosen modular seating units, low cube tables, a console table, a dining table, and four pull-up chairs. (There is only one dining table, but it is shown with its leaves up and down.)

3. Cut out the furniture places from your first copy. Arrange them on the plan suitable for a *quiet dinner and evening of reading and music for two people*. When you have an arrangement that satisfies you, glue the furniture pieces onto the plan.

4. Cut out the furniture pieces from your second copy. Arrange them on the plan suitably for a party at which *eight people will watch a football game on television and have a buffet supper*. When you have an arrangement that satisfies you, glue the furniture pieces onto the plan.

5. Cut out the furniture pieces from your third copy. Arrange them on the plan suitably for a *dancing party of twenty people*. When you have an arrangement that satisfies you, glue the furniture pieces onto the plan.

Consider

A well-planned group space should be flexible enough to accommodate many types of activities. Modular furniture makes rearrangement easy, but different functions could also be served with more conventional pieces.

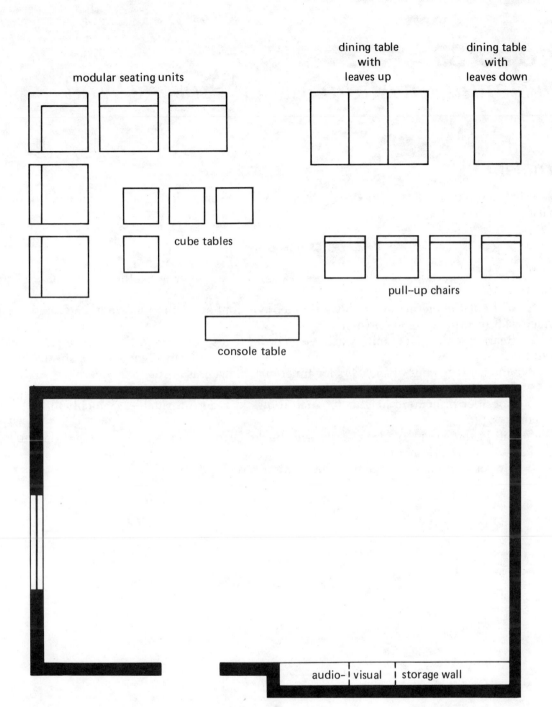

modular seating units

dining table
with
leaves up

dining table
with
leaves down

cube tables

pull-up chairs

console table

audio-visual | storage wall

living/dining room

Project 39
Designing an Audio-Visual Storage Wall

Problem

To design a sophisticated audio-visual storage wall accommodating all the various equipment available.

Procedure

1. Draw an elevation of a wall, either in your own home or in another household, using the scale $1'' = 1'$.

2. Cut out the pictures of audio and video equipment on the following page, and design a storage wall incorporating all of them.

3. Rearrange the pieces until you have an order that satisfies you. For video equipment, you should consider viewing heights. Without getting too deeply involved in acoustical problems, consider the arrangement of speakers for functional as well as aesthetic concerns.

4. Include storage for records and tapes.

5. Consider placement heights for such things as record turntables, which will be handled constantly.

6. Fill in the spaces between units with books, artifacts, or whatever items you choose.

7. Paste the equipment onto your drawing. Sketch in the other elements.

8. Mount the finished design on illustration board.

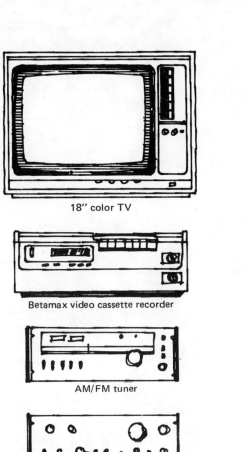

18" color TV

Betamax video cassette recorder

AM/FM tuner

integrated amplifier

time delay system

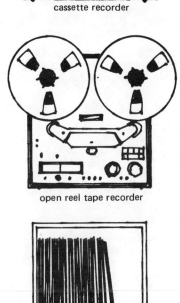

dynamic range expander

turntable

cassette recorder

open reel tape recorder

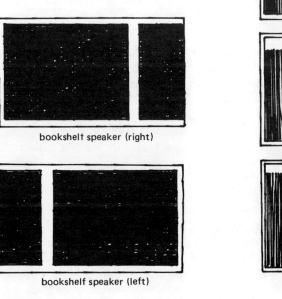

bookshelf speaker (right)

bookshelf speaker (left)

records

Private Places

13

Privacy is a necessity. Individuals require different degrees of privacy for sleeping, dressing, and bathing. Other kinds of private spaces must be established when overnight guests visit the home or when a member of the household pursues tasks that demand seclusion. Most importantly, though, human beings need and desire spaces in which to collect their thoughts and dream their dreams, to get to know themselves as people.

Several factors challenge the quest for privacy, foremost among them the very existence of increasing numbers of people concentrated in increasingly smaller areas. Most households today probably cannot afford to provide individual rooms or suites for each member. Nevertheless, with intelligent planning we can design homes that offer each inhabitant a private space in which to retreat.

A well-designed bedroom affords a quiet retreat at any time of the day. It can be relaxing to curl up or stretch out on a bed during the afternoon. Often, bedrooms provide the best conditions in the home for concentrated reading, study, or meditation.

In designing a bedroom, one must take two major factors into account: the number of people who will occupy the room and their ages; and the various roles the room will have to play. Particularly when space is limited, the amount of room available may be a major factor in planning a sleeping area.

Children and young people especially enjoy rooms that have much free floor space and surfaces on which things can be displayed. There must be room for the imagination, room to move, lots of storage that the *child* can reach—everything, in fact, scaled to the child. If possible, the child should choose the colors.

As always, design decisions must be based on the people who will actually live in the home.

Project 40
Designing a Bedroom for Privacy and Sound Insulation

Problem

To design a bedroom for two people, allowing them privacy from each other and insulation from sound generated in adjacent rooms.

Procedure

1. Draw a floor plan of a relatively large bedroom—perhaps 18′ × 24′, in the scale ¼″ = 1′. Roughly indicate a social space abutting one short wall of the room, and a hallway running the length of one long wall.

2. Assume that the bedroom will be occupied by two people—either siblings or roommates.

3. Working with the furniture shapes on page 97, design a room that will afford sound insulation *and* privacy for each of the two people. Each person should be provided with a bed, desk, chest of drawers, closet, table, and chair.

4. Consider various possibilities for sound insulation and privacy. Examples would be a storage unit on the wall abutting the social space, a storage wall between halves of the room, partial walls, and fabrics utilized for both purposes.

5. When you have decided upon the arrangement of furniture, glue or trace the furniture outlines on your plan.

6. Sketch in the other elements needed for privacy or sound insulation.

Consider

Each person in the room should have the opportunity to get *completely* away from the other when this is desirable. You may, however, want to provide for some shared, communal space in the room.

Project 41
Designing a Child's Bedroom

Problem

To design a bedroom that meets the needs and desires of a real child, aged 6 to 12.

Procedure

1. Find a real child, aged 6 to 12, whom you can interview. Begin to plan a bedroom based on that child's preferences.

2. Show the child examples of colors, and ask him or her to pick two or three that he or she likes best.

3. Find out how the child would like to sleep—in a bunk bed, regular bed, platform bed. Does the child ever have playmates spend the night?

4. What are the child's favorite games or toys, and does he or she play with them in the bedroom?

5. Would the child enjoy a swing, punching bag, or gymnastic equipment in the bedroom?

6. Does the child have a pet that spends all or part of the time in the bedroom?

7. Does the child like to draw and display finished work?

8. Does the child have collections of objects?

9. When you have discovered the answers to these questions, sketch a room plan based on the child's preferences.

Consider

Even if the child's expressed preferences seem outrageous, there may be a way to accommodate them partially, without compromising the values of the parents. This room is meant to be the child's own private place, and his or her individuality should be considered. Beware, however, of transitory wishes; a child of six will grow into a child of seven, and may want quite different things.

Work Spaces

14

The work spaces of the home include the kitchen, laundry area, and such other specialized places as workshop and sewing room. Because it is so universal and so central to our everyday lives, the kitchen has received the most attention. Designers and efficiency experts have outdone each other in trying to create the most beautiful, functional spaces in which to prepare food.

There are many technical studies of kitchen efficiency. Most of them involve work curves and walking patterns (least amount of arm movement, least amount of space between appliances). All of these considerations are important, perhaps more today than ever before, when it is no longer deemed appropriate for the "housewife" to spend most of the day in the kitchen. For those who enjoy cooking, kitchen planning may involve eliminating the "chore" aspects so as to allow maximum room for creativeness. For those who detest cooking, design should revolve around getting the task done as quickly and painlessly as possible. In either case, a well-planned kitchen can be a blessing.

Project 42
Transforming a Badly Designed Kitchen

Problem

To redesign a kitchen that does not "work" because of faulty placement of appliances, inadequate counter space, poor work curves, and awkward traffic patterns.

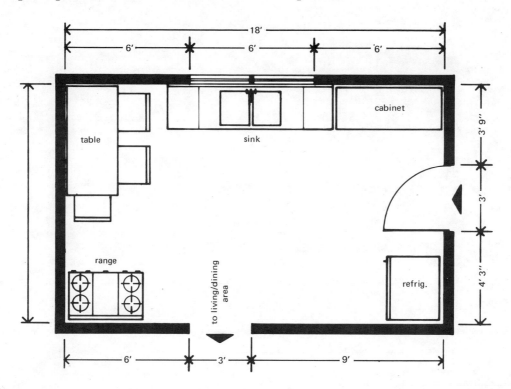

Procedure

1. The kitchen plan shown on this page could be found in many an older home today. Study the arrangement of elements. List on a piece of paper all the things you can find wrong with this kitchen.

2. Trace the outline of the floor plan on a piece of graph paper. Include the window and both doors.

3. Trace or photocopy the appliances and furnishings, using the symbols on page 94.

4. Cut out the symbols, and arrange them on the floor plan according to a more efficient pattern. For this exercise, do not worry about plumbing, electric, or gas hookups. Move the appliances freely to achieve the best pattern.

5. Add extra cabinets, counters, or furnishings as you consider necessary, leaving the basic refrigerator, sink, and cooking surface, of course.

6. When you have arrived at an arrangement that pleases you, paste the cutouts onto the plan.

Consider

Why does this kitchen "work" better now? Analyze the work curves, traffic patterns, and placement on your new plan.

Project 43
Household Maintenance

Problem

To determine how much time is presently spent on household maintenance, and how this time could be lessened.

Procedure

   1. Fill out the housekeeping chart on the next page, listing all the household chores done in a single week. If you yourself do no housekeeping chores, find someone who does, and ask that person to fill out the chart.
   2. List the amount of time spent on each chore, and put a check mark according to whether you enjoyed the task, tolerated it, or actively hated doing it. (See the partially filled-out example below.)
   3. In the last column, suggest ways the task could be eased or even eliminated.

Consider

You may want to ask each member of the household to fill out a chart. This is a graphic way of seeing who does what around the house. Perhaps a hated task now done by one member could be taken over by another who may tolerate or even enjoy it.

Day	Task	Time spent	Enjoyed it	Didn't mind it	Hated it	How could this task be lessened or eliminated?
Monday	washed breakfast dishes	15 min.		✓		
	swept floor	10 min.			✓	Better doormat outside kitchen door
	washed clothes	2 hrs.		✓		
	ironed clothes	1½ hrs.			✓	Buy more no-iron clothes. Send more to cleaners. Have everyone iron their own!
Tuesday	washed breakfast dishes	15 min.		✓		
	Cooked dinner	1 hr.	✓			
Wednesday	washed breakfast dishes	15 min.		✓		
	Grocery shopped + put groceries away	2 hrs. ½ hr.	✓		✓	no counter by refrigerator.. need one for setting things on temporarily
Thursday	washed breakfast dishes	15 min.			✓	Easier if we had comforters instead of blankets and spreads.
	made beds	20 min.			✓	

Housekeeping Chart

Day	Task	Time spent	Enjoyed it	Didn't mind it	Hated it	How could this task be lessened or eliminated?

The Personal Home: Accessories

15

The term accessories includes most of the additional furnishings needed to make a home livable in all senses. Many people think of an "accessory" as something subordinate. Subordinate calls to mind a collection of small, dispensible objects used for their decorative appeal—if any. We prefer to think of accessories as supplementary, "something that completes."

Many of the functional accessories, such as china and silver, fall outside the province of the professional designer. Often, they are acquired by inheritance or gift. A typical household will have several sets of tableware and bedding. Since they are out of sight much of the time, they do not play a permanent role in the overall design of the interior.

Far more crucial to the visual success of a design are the art objects that embellish a room. Their selection depends on the tastes of the household members. Their arrangement can be an art in itself. That is the subject of the project in this section.

Project 44
Arranging Art on a Wall

Problem

To make a well-designed arrangement of paintings, prints, and drawings on the wall space above a sofa.

Procedure

1. Make tracings or photocopies of the pictures opposite, and try them in different groupings on the wall elevation on page 84. Try to use at least seven of the works.

2. When you find a grouping you like, paste it down.

Consider

To achieve a satisfactory grouping, you must keep in mind the relationship of each picture to the total arrangement, and the arrangement's relationship to the height and width of the wall, as well as to the furniture below. In general:

Visually "heavy" pictures should be interspersed with lighter ones, so the weight of the composition is even. Heavier pictures are usually placed nearer the bottom of the composition to give it stability.

Keep the distance between pictures less than the height of each picture for a feeling of unity.

Distribute the sizes of the pictures, rather than having all small ones together and all large together.

Unity will be simplified if the overall composition forms a rectangle, and if the four corners are established first.

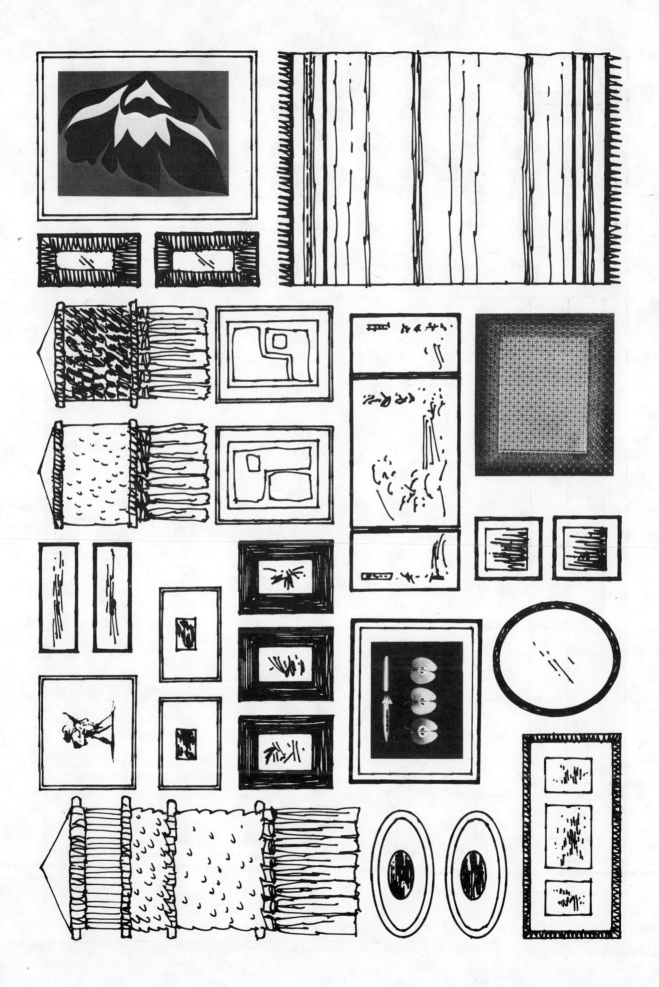

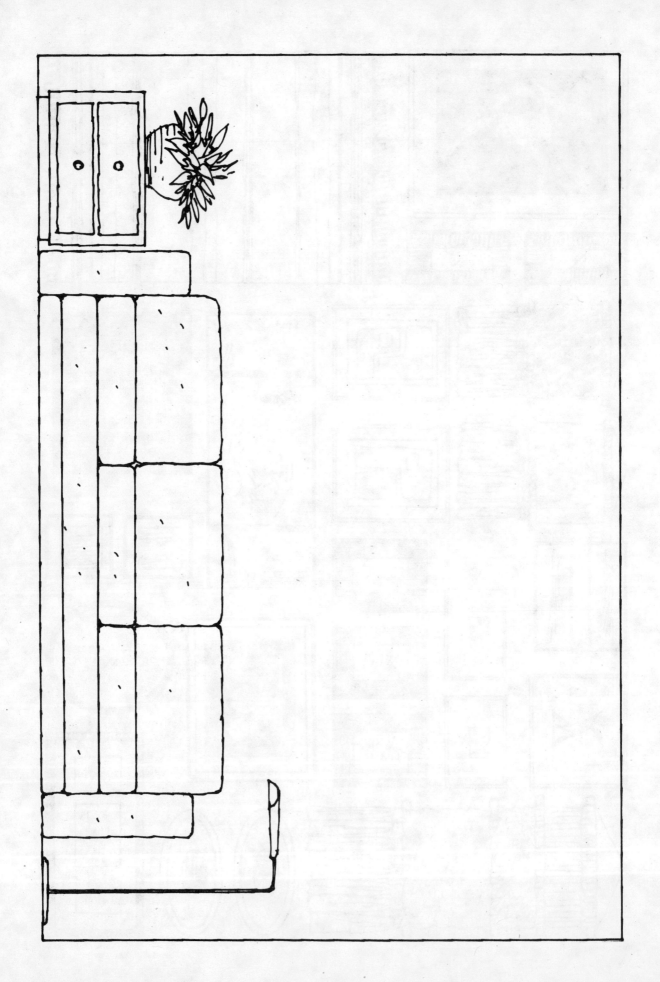

Costs and Budgets

16

Costs and budgets mark neither the beginning nor the end of the interior design process; they are factors to be considered throughout. The price tags on home furnishings are sometimes determined by materials and construction, excellence and individuality of design, and durability. But often they are simply determined by what is "in" at the moment, or by supply and demand. Good design can be created for any budget. The ingenuity of the designer is more important than the cost of furnishings and materials.

Alternatives to buying new furniture exist for people who are willing and able to spend the time "scavenging"—that is, collecting old furniture for nothing or next to nothing and fixing it up. Also, for those who have the talent, unique interiors can be created by assembling your own furnishings. Today, this does not mean the use of wood alone. Many new home furnishings are being made from materials that had previously been used only in industry: corrugated cardboard, plastic webbing, metal shelving systems, scaffolding, parachutes, safety glass, movers' pads, and steel deck plates.

If these examples seem too extreme, but your budget is nevertheless limited, planned buying may be the answer. The acquisition of furnishings over a period of time should be planned at least as wisely as color schemes and furniture arrangements. A sensible approach suggests buying the large essential pieces first, then filling in gradually with smaller items and embellishments. This procedure forces you (or your client) to compare present life style to that which will prevail in the future. Planned buying should be flexible enough to evolve with future tastes and incomes, and designed so that the best use is made of furniture already chosen.

Project 45
Planned Buying

Problem

To plan the purchase of furnishings for a small apartment, over a period of two years.

Procedure

1. Assume you are about to move into a small apartment, consisting of a living room, dining L, bedroom, and efficiency kitchen (no room in the kitchen for furniture). You have no possessions except your clothing, books, and miscellaneous artifacts.

2. Assume further that you have $2500 now; will have an additional $2500 a year from now; and will have a third $2500 two years from now.

3. From the list, choose the items you will buy immediately, to make your apartment livable and functional. The total of your purchase may not exceed $2500.

4. From the list, choose the items you will buy a year from now, not exceeding $2500.

5. From the list, choose the items you will buy two years from now, not exceeding $2500.

Consider

The "most important" things to buy are an individual choice. You may decide to splurge $2000 on the Oriental rug or the painting, buy a sleeping bag, a chair, and a lamp, and eat out. You may choose to buy only a few "good" things that will last a lifetime; or to spend your money on many cheap things that can be discarded later when you can afford better. Keep in mind what is best for *you.*

Living Room	Dining Area	Bedroom
sofa $500	small table $200	innerspring set $350
sofa-bed $700	large table $800	headboard/footboard $300
modular units $300 each	chairs $100 each	platform bed $200
easy chair $400	server $450	waterbed $800
recliner $500		sleeping bag $150
director's chair $50		metal frame for mattress $25
wicker chair $75		table lamp $75
dining table $400		wall lamp $100
coffee table $75		chest of drawers $200
stacking boxes $30 each		stacking boxes $30 each
television set $600		bookcase $300
stereo $600		wall-to-wall carpeting $700
desk $500		area rugs $75 each
bookcase $300		sheets $20 each
poster $10		pillows $45 each
curtains $200		bedspread $150
draperies $500		cotton throw $50
shelving $35 per shelf		shelving $35 per shelf
floor lamp $150		chair $150
table lamps $75 each		curtains $100
track lighting $100		draperies $300
wall-to-wall carpeting $900		
Oriental rug $2000		
area rugs $75 each		
painting $2000		
print $250		
reproduction $20		

Profile Questionnaire

I. People

1. Who will live in the home?

a. *Adults:* number _____ approximate ages _____ special needs _____
b. *Teens / young adults:* number _____ approximate ages _____ special needs _____
c. *Children:* number _____ ages by sex _____ special needs _____
d. *Elderly / handicapped people:* special needs _____
e. *Pets:* number _____ kind(s) _____ size(s) _____ special needs _____ outside
   only _____ inside _____
f. *Guests:* occasional _____ frequent _____ long visits _____ short visits _____ mainly
   relatives _____ mainly friends _____
Do they become members of the family? _____
Or are they more formally treated? _____
g. *Other:* boarders _____ live-in help _____
Do you expect the composition of the household to change in the next five years? _____ ten
   years? _____ children will be added _____ grown children will leave _____ adult
   relatives will move in _____
   explain: _____

II. Life Style

1. What type of home do you live in?
one room _____ apartment _____ house _____ mobile home _____ other _____
own the home _____ rent _____ board _____

1. How do you like to live?
casually _____ informally _____ formally _____ inexpensively _____
   moderately _____ luxuriously _____

3. How do you like to entertain?
a. *Casually:* never _____ infrequently _____ occasionally _____ often _____
b. *Informally:* never _____ infrequently _____ occasionally _____ often _____
c. *Formally:* never _____ infrequently _____ occasionally _____ often _____

4. What do you do for entertainment in the home?
a. *Talk:* in living room _____ family room _____ kitchen _____ outdoor terrace,
   porch _____ other _____
b. *Read:* in solitude _____ in a social group _____ aloud _____ in living room _____
   family room _____ bedroom(s) _____ study _____ other _____
c. *Watch television:* in living room _____ family room _____ bedroom(s) _____
   kitchen _____
How many television sets do you need? _____
Should television be segregated from other activities? _____
d. *Listen to music:* radio _____ where? _____ stereo _____ where? _____
How much stereo equipment must be accommodated? _____
Is placement of components for good listening important? _____
Do you need storage space for records and tapes? _____
e. *Play music:* piano _____ portable instruments _____ drums _____ amplification
   equipment _____
Where will music be played? _____
Will the instrument(s) be used for practice? _____
Or will they be used for entertainment only? _____
f. *Games and active play:* bridge _____ backgammon _____ other board games _____
   played regularly _____ occasionally _____ never _____

Do you like a permanent card table _____ folding card table _____
Or do you use the dining table _____ coffee table _____ floor _____
Do you need space for active indoor play (dancing, billiards, ping-pong, etc)?
    Type and location_____
Do you need space for outdoor sports? Type and location _____
Do you need to provide for children's play? _____ indoors: bedrooms _____ family
    room _____ outdoors: play yard _____ lawn _____

5. What are your eating habits?

a. *Place for meals* (percent of time): living room _____ living-dining room _____ dining
    room _____ kitchen _____ living-kitchen _____ family room _____ outdoor
    terrace _____ restaurants _____ in various places, according to people and
    occasion _____
b. *Types of meals* (percent of time): pot-luck _____ casual _____ on the run _____
    informal _____ buffet _____ sit-down _____ formal _____
Does everyone eat together? _____
    How often and where are snacks eaten?_____

6. What kind of cooking facilities do you like?

very simple _____ average _____ elaborate _____
separate kitchen _____ living-kitchen _____ living area _____ outdoor barbecue _____
Do two or more people often cook at the same time? _____
Do you have a large library of cookbooks? _____
Do you have any specialties (such as baking) that would benefit from having separate
    facilities? _____

7. What is your approach to housekeeping?

wary _____ resigned _____ average _____ compulsive _____
Who is responsible for cleaning the home? everyone _____ one adult _____
    all adults _____ teenagers _____ children _____ hired help _____
Where is most of your laundry done? wash basin _____ in-home washer/dryer _____
    laundromat _____ apartment washer/dryer _____ commercial service _____

8. What kinds of hobbies do you have?

large-scale _____ small-scale _____ quiet _____ noisy _____
    special needs _____

9. Do you have any collections that should be accommodated or displayed?

    special needs _____

10. Do you work at home?

desk work _____
    other _____
    special needs (desk, files, drawing table, typewriter, etc.)
    _____

11. What are your personal habits?

a. *Smoking.* Do you smoke? _____
Do other members of the household smoke? _____
Do you permit guests to smoke in your home? _____
Should smoking be segregated in one room or section of the home? _____
Should furnishings and colors be selected so as not to show the effects of smoke? _____
Or would you tolerate the extra maintenance involved so as to enjoy light colors and
    fabrics? _____
b. *Drinking:*
Do you enjoy soft drinks or alcoholic beverages? seldom _____ occasionally _____
    often _____
Do you serve beverages to guests? seldom _____ occasionally _____ often _____
Would you like provision for a separate bar or drink caddy: in living room _____ in family
    room _____ in kitchen _____ outdoors _____ portable _____

c. *Communication:*
How important to you is the telephone? very _____ somewhat _____ not at all _____
In which rooms would you like to have a telephone? kitchen _____ living room _____
    bedroom(s) _____ family room _____ bathroom _____ outdoors _____
    other _____

III. Mobility

1. How long will you live in your present home?
less than five years _____ five to ten years _____ indefinitely _____

2. How will you move?
alone _____ with help from family and friends _____ professional mover for large
    items _____ for everything _____

3. Where will you move?
to a different dwelling _____ to a different community _____ to a different climate _____
    to a different country _____

4. Do you or will you have a second home? _____
Will each be completely furnished? _____
Will you move some furnishings between the two places (television set, sleeping bags,
    knock-down furniture)? _____

IV. Location, Climate, and Orientation

1. Where do you live?
city _____ suburb _____ country _____
cold climate _____ warm climate _____ temperate climate _____ dry climate _____
    damp climate _____

2. Do you have pleasant views?
from all windows _____ from some windows _____ not at all _____

3. Do you need to provide privacy?
during the day _____ at night _____ always _____

4. Do you need to provide for insulation against heat and cold?
too much sun _____ too little sun _____ cold winds _____

V. Proxemics—Response to Space and People

1. How do you respond to space?
Do you feel the need for space in which to spread out? physically _____ visually _____
Do you like to feel enclosed and protected? physically _____ visually _____

2. How do you respond to people?
Do you like to be in physical contact, even if only casually? _____
Or do you prefer visual contact without physical contact? _____
Do you have varying needs according to moods or work? _____
Do you like to be alone: most of the time _____ often _____ occasionally _____
    never _____ hate it _____
Do you like to be part of a group: most of the time _____ often _____ occasionally _____
    never _____ hate it _____

3. Is most of your day spent: outside the home _____
    in noisy group situations _____ in quiet groups _____
    at home, mostly alone _____ with young children _____

VI. Light and Color

1. Natural light:
Do you seek sun _____ or shade _____
Does daylight make you feel energetic? _____
Do you have any problems related to amount of light? _____

2. Artificial lighting:
Do you prefer: indirect, even lighting _____ dramatic, focused lighting _____
Do you need special lighting for certain tasks? _____

3. Color:
How do you respond to color? slightly _____ moderately _____ strongly _____
Do colors affect and/or express your moods? _____
Do you like a lot of color? _____ or restraint? _____
Do you like colors that are:

bright _____ clear _____ dominant _____ clashing _____ deep _____
rich _____ intense _____ positive _____ exuberant _____ dark _____
glowing _____ mellow _____ delicate _____ light _____ soft _____
subdued _____ cool _____ variegated _____ contrasting _____ raw _____
monochromatic _____ neutral _____

VII. Taste and Personality

1. Are your clothes: tailored _____ trim _____
neat _____ casual _____ thrown together _____ comfortable above all _____
flowing _____ relaxed _____ conservative _____ wild _____
Do you like to keep up with the latest styles? _____
Or do you stay with styles that suit you? _____

2. Do you consider your personality to be: forceful _____
shy _____ boisterous _____ quiet _____ romantic _____ sensible _____
worldly _____

3. What does a home mean to you?
Check each of the following values that you would like your home to express or foster:

prestige _____ aesthetics _____ conformity _____ nonconformity _____
security _____ independence _____ comfort _____ nature _____ privacy _____
sociability _____ leisure _____ achievement _____ family ties _____
economy _____ serenity _____ convenience _____ eccentricity _____

4. What do you want for your home?
already know _____ have seen exactly what you want _____ want to explore the
possibilities _____ would like a professional to suggest solutions _____ like
tried-and-true solutions _____ like to experiment _____

5. Who will make the design decisions?
Will you, as an individual, make all the decisions for the household? _____
Will other members of the household participate in the actual design process?
husband or wife _____ children _____ roommate _____
Will a professional designer assume full control? _____
other_____

6. Style
Does the architecture of your home follow a certain style? _____
Do you want the interior to follow the same style? _____
Must everything conform to the same style? _____
Or would you like to mix styles and periods, choosing individual pieces that you like?
_____

Can you envision a mixture that would be compatible (lively but not chaotic)?
_____

Do you want to evolve your own style to express you and your life style?
_____

VIII. Resources

1. Inventory your present possessions:

	have sufficient	need or want to replace
beds		
chests		
chairs		
sofas		
coffee tables		
side tables		
lounge chairs		
pull-up chairs		
dining table		
dining chairs		
cabinets for china, glass, silverware		
bookcases		
carpets		
area rugs		
curtains		
draperies		
window shades		
lamps		
works of art		
range		
oven(s)		
refrigerator		
dishwasher		
trash compactor		
kitchen tools		
clothes washer		
clothes dryer		
ironing board		

2. What will you need to buy right away? _____
What can wait until a year from now? _____
   five years from now? _____

3. How much money do you have?
The budget is: skimpy _____ enough for basics _____ ample _____ the sky's the limit _____
The money: is at hand _____ will be available for the first year _____ will be available over a five-year period _____ will be available later _____

4. What abilities or skills do you have?
a. *Sewing* (curtains, upholstery, etc.) _____
b. *Weaving* or other fabrication techniques _____
c. *Carpentry:* small repairs _____ putting up bookshelves _____ making furniture _____ skilled cabinetwork _____
d. *Painting:* furniture _____ walls _____ anything _____
e. *Other:* _____

5. How much money do you want to spend on upkeep?

minimum _____ average _____ no limit _____

How much time do you want to spend on upkeep? minimum _____ average _____ no limit _____

6. Are you concerned about conservation of energy and natural resources?

Which of the following would you like to explore:

solar energy _____

noncentral heating (wood-burning stove, etc.) _____

insulation against heat and/or cold _____

recycling _____

biodegradability _____

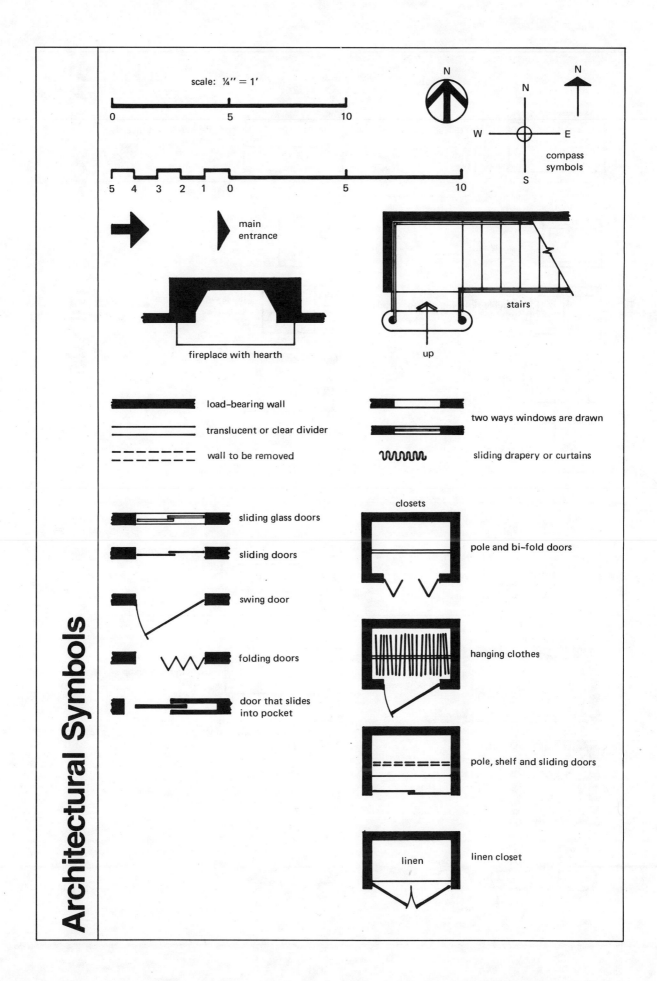

scale: ¼″ = 1′

compass symbols

main entrance

fireplace with hearth

stairs

up

load–bearing wall

translucent or clear divider

wall to be removed

two ways windows are drawn

sliding drapery or curtains

sliding glass doors

sliding doors

swing door

folding doors

door that slides into pocket

closets

pole and bi–fold doors

hanging clothes

pole, shelf and sliding doors

linen closet

linen

Architectural Symbols

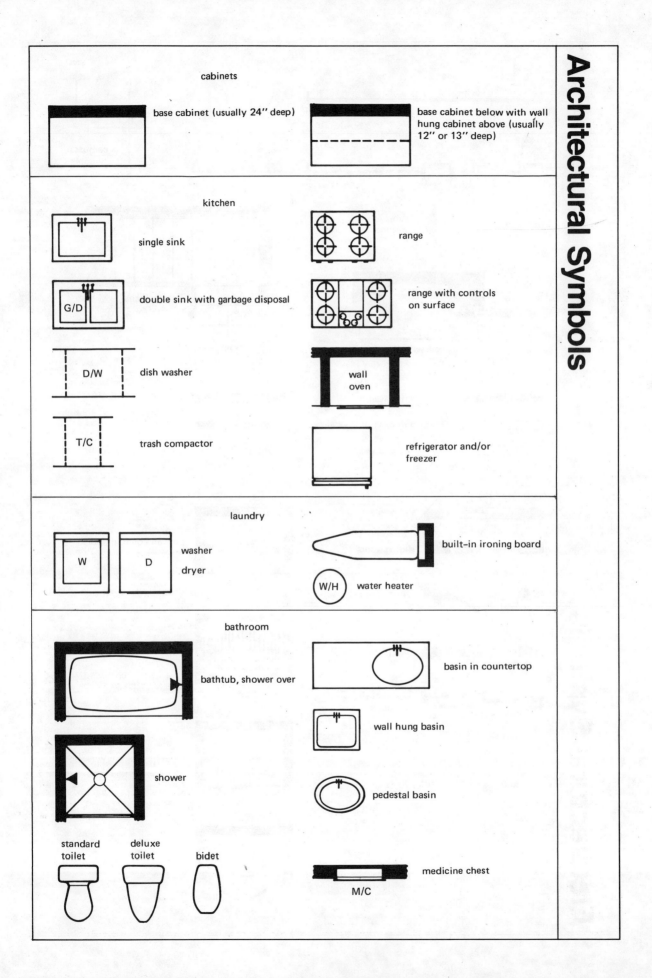

cabinets

base cabinet (usually 24" deep)

base cabinet below with wall hung cabinet above (usually 12" or 13" deep)

kitchen

single sink

range

double sink with garbage disposal

G/D

range with controls on surface

D/W

dish washer

wall oven

T/C

trash compactor

refrigerator and/or freezer

laundry

W

D

washer

dryer

built–in ironing board

W/H

water heater

bathroom

bathtub, shower over

basin in countertop

wall hung basin

shower

pedestal basin

standard toilet

deluxe toilet

bidet

medicine chest

M/C

wall light		ceiling light	
pull chain wall light		recessed ceiling light	
switch		heat light	
3–way switch		ceiling fan	
thermostat		pull chain ceiling light	
110 volt outlet		track lighting	
220 volt outlet		surface individual fluorescent	
special outlet (air-conditioner) 20 amps		recessed individual fluorescent	
clock outlet		surface continuous row fluorescent	
floor electric outlet		recessed continuous row fluorescent	
telephone outlet			
floor telephone outlet		floor and table lamps	
television antennae outlet			
door bell			
controls one fixture		two 3-way switches control two lights	
controls one fixture and one outlet			

Electrical Symbols

Lighting for Activities Chart		
Room or area		
Window direction		
Daylight controlled by:		
Activities		
	Day	
	Night	
	Both	
Mood desired		
Lighting needed	General	Direct
		Indirect
	Local	Task
		Decorative

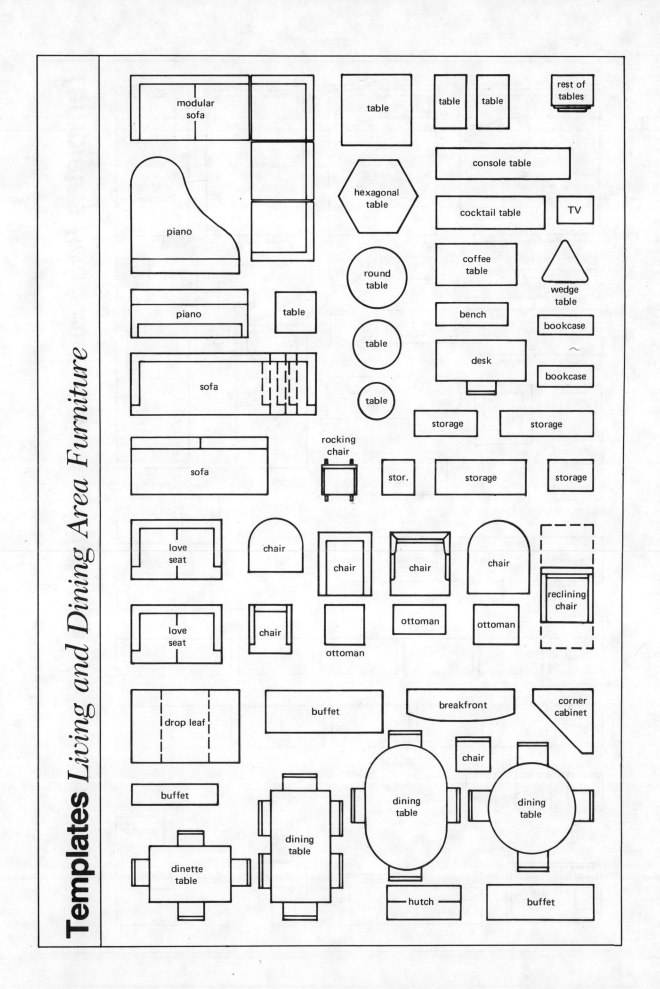

Templates *Living and Dining Area Furniture*

modular sofa

piano

piano

sofa

sofa

table

table

table

rest of tables

hexagonal table

round table

table

table

console table

cocktail table

TV

coffee table

wedge table

bench

bookcase

desk

bookcase

storage

storage

stor.

storage

storage

rocking chair

love seat

love seat

chair

chair

chair

chair

chair

chair

ottoman

ottoman

ottoman

reclining chair

drop leaf

buffet

breakfront

corner cabinet

buffet

chair

dinette table

dining table

dining table

dining table

hutch

buffet

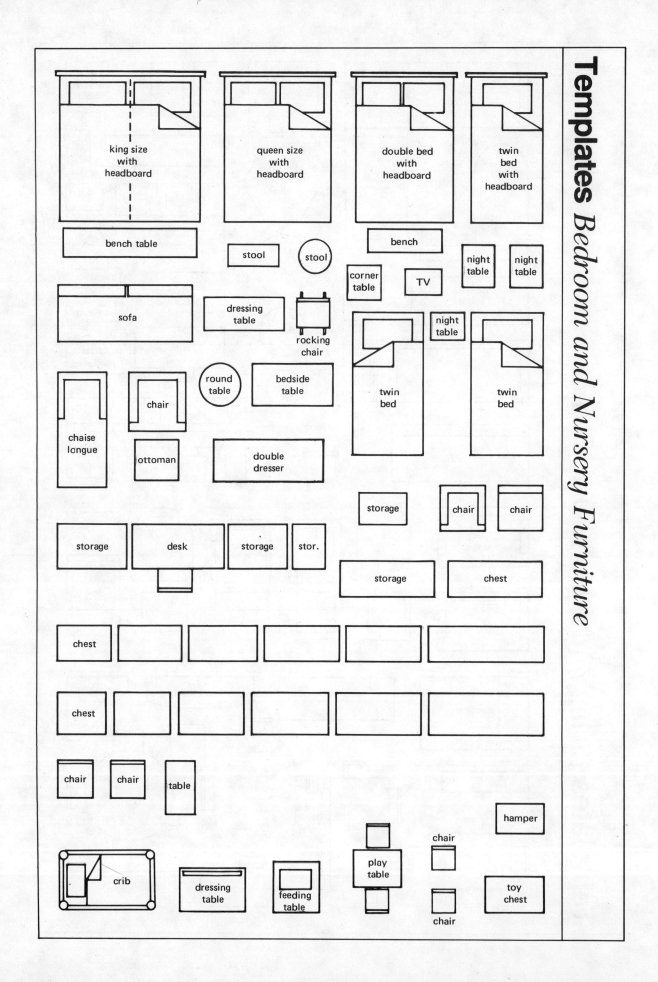

king size with headboard

queen size with headboard

double bed with headboard

twin bed with headboard

bench table

stool

stool

bench

corner table

TV

night table

night table

sofa

dressing table

rocking chair

night table

twin bed

twin bed

chaise longue

chair

round table

bedside table

ottoman

double dresser

storage

chair

chair

storage

storage

desk

storage

stor.

storage

chest

chest

chest

chair

chair

table

hamper

play table

chair

crib

dressing table

feeding table

chair

toy chest